# ORIGAMI
## A COMPLETE
## STEP-BY-STEP
## GUIDE

Be properly
addressed!
POSTCODE

SOUTHGATE
9 JAN
1989
N.14

Mick Morley
21 Hardwicke Rd
London
N13 4SL

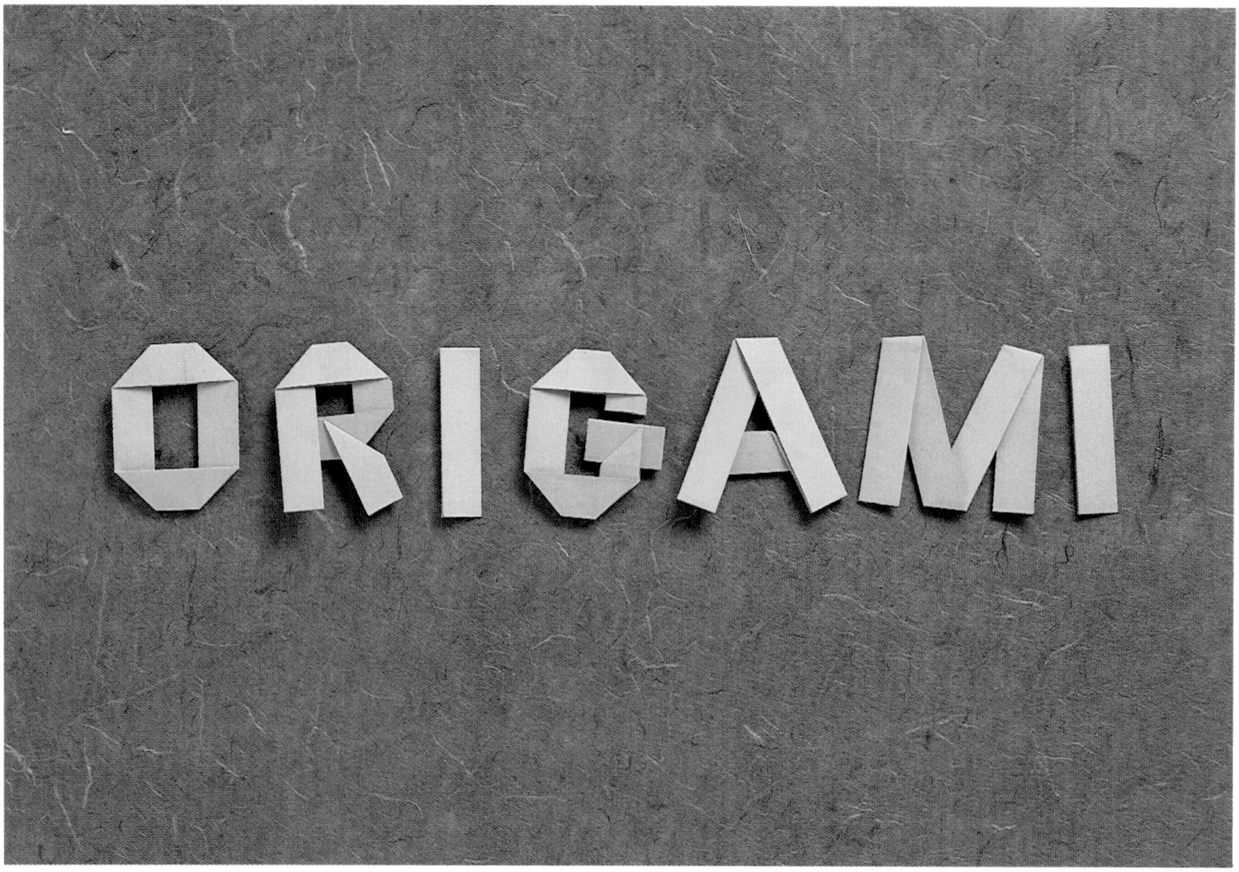
ORIGAMI

# ORIGAMI
## A COMPLETE STEP-BY-STEP GUIDE

PAUL JACKSON

HAMLYN

This edition published in 1989 by
The Hamlyn Publishing Group Limited,
a division of the Octopus Publishing Group,
Michelin House,
81 Fulham Road,
London SW3 6RB

ISBN 0 600 565 483

Produced by Mandarin Offset — printed in Hong Kong


ACKNOWLEDGMENTS
**Editor** Mary-Clare Jerram
**Art Editor** Bob Gordon
**Copy Editor** Suzy Powling
**Designer** Patrick Nugent
**Production Controller** Garry Lewis
**Photographer** Mark Harwood
**Artists** Anthony Duke, Steve Pearse, Dave Sexton

# CONTENTS

| | |
|---|---|
| How to use this book | 6 |
| About origami | 7 |
| Papers | 8 |
| **Getting started** | **11** |
| How to make a square | 12 |
| Starting to fold | 15 |
| How to follow the diagrams | 20 |
| **Valley/mountain designs** | **23** |
| Chinese glider | 25 |
| Multi box | 27 |
| Swan | 33 |
| Christmas decoration | 36 |
| Fan | 38 |
| Back-to-front serviette | 40 |
| Letterfold | 42 |
| Flying eagle | 43 |
| Pistol | 46 |
| Japanese box | 48 |
| Robot | 51 |
| Santa Claus | 57 |
| Mouse | 60 |
| Bracelet | 62 |
| Weave patterns | 64 |
| Goldfish | 68 |

ORIGAMI

**Squash fold designs**   **71**
Puppy   75
Crown   78
Flower   80
False nose and
   moustache   82
Strawberry   84

**Inside and outside
   reverse fold designs**   **87**
Four feeding birds   93
Snail   95
Butterfly ring   96
Monkeys   98
Reverse fold
   alphabet   100
Six-pointed star   105
Fallen leaves   108

**Petal fold designs**   **109**
Two flapping birds   113
Moustache   115
Pentagonal flower   118

**Pre-crease designs**   **121**
Bookmark   122
Cubic box   123
Bugatti   125

**Sink fold designs**   **131**
Three boats   136
Hyperbolic parabola   138
Ten-pointed star   142

**Projects**   **145**
Sprung frame   146
Heads   148
Yacht   150
Octagonal flower
   and stem   152
Keys on a ring   155
Mouse   161
Cassette case   163
Sweet dish   166
Spectacles   168
Sleigh   170

Table of symbols   173
Acknowledgments   176

ORIGAMI

# HOW TO USE THIS BOOK

U nlike previously published books on origami, this one is a complete course on paperfolding. It begins by carefully explaining the rudiments of folding, then takes the reader through the basic techniques and ends with a chapter of difficult designs. Each chapter presents a new technique illustrated with exercises and designs to fold.

To get the most pleasure from the book, it is important to start at the beginning. You are advised not to jump backwards and forwards too much unless you can follow the instructions without much guidance. If you do not want to make all the designs in every chapter, at least make the basic examples and do the exercises so that you are familiar with the techniques. Learn the symbols and refer to the Table of symbols at the back if you forget what they mean.

Not everyone will be able to fold the more complex designs. For this reason, the opening chapter of valley/mountain designs is extended so that the less able student can fold a lot of simple designs and appreciate the pleasures of folding paper.

Before starting to fold, read the introductory sections giving advice on which papers to use and explaining the best methods of folding.

When you come to the end of this book, you may want to find out more about origami. Most libraries and book shops stock books on the subject. However, be careful. Some of the books are badly written and should be avoided. Disregard those which cannot explain simple designs in a simple way. Avoid books for children written in poor English which look as if they came from the Far East. The designs are usually very complicated and badly explained.

Thankfully, though, there are a large number of wonderful origami books, many in English, by authors such as Harbin, Kenneway and Randlett. More and more books are being published and the standard is consistently high. Some contain a large number of very complex designs so if you want to make simple models, sift through the pages with care.

Japanese and Oriental import shops in large cities often sell very good books, usually in Japanese. Remember that even though the language may be foreign, the symbols are the same as in English books, so you should be able to follow the instructions. Ask for books by Yoshizawa, Kasahara, Takahama, Momotani or Fuse. They are all superb and some are in English translations.

If you want to join a club, two addresses of origami societies are given below. They are both friendly, inexpensive and cater well for the inexperienced enthusiast. The BOS in Britain is more international than the Friends in the United States, and is a major publishing house for new designs, information and theory. The Friends are concerned more with the learning and teaching of origami. Both organize annual conventions, send out informative newsletters and carry a wide range of books and papers for sale to members only.

**The British Origami Society**
253 Park Lane
Poynton
Cheshire SK12 1RH

**The Friends of the Origami Center of America**
15 West 77th Street
New York City
NY 10024
USA

# ABOUT ORIGAMI

The art of paperfolding begins with the invention of paper. The Chinese were the first to make paper, certainly during the 2nd century AD and perhaps before, but no folded designs have survived from these earliest times. The process of papermaking remained a secret until the Chinese invaded Korea, and later Japan, in 610 AD, after which the knowledge spread westwards through Asia and the Middle East, eventually reaching Europe in about 1150.

The Japanese quickly refined and extended the process of making paper until the material became an integral part of their everyday lives. There has been much speculation as to why this was so. It has been suggested that the humidity of the Japanese islands is particularly favourable to the drying of paper; other possible contributory factors include its soft water, the availability of particular reeds and bushes with remarkably long fibres which bond to form very strong paper, the lack of other natural resources on the islands with which to make clothes, sacks, screens and other essentials and the enthusiasm of the Japanese people for intense physical activity (papermaking can be exhausting). Whatever the reasons for its adoption by the Japanese, paper became and remains more important and more revered than it has ever been in the West.

The oldest known designs of folded paper are of Japanese origin, from an uncertain date before 1000 AD, perhaps much earlier. Several dozen designs have survived into the modern era and were important in establishing the basic vocabulary of the art. In acknowledgment of this, Western paperfolders have adopted the Japanese word 'origami' for their art.

For several generations, however, between the mid-1800s and the 1930s, origami almost became a lost art. The imposition of Western values on Japanese culture, brought about through Japan's new policy of open trade, meant that many indigenous arts declined. Origami survived by mothers teaching it to their children, but the symbolic meanings behind many of the designs were lost and origami became no more than an amusement.

In the West, simple folded shapes had been known for many years, perhaps even for centuries; no one can be sure. The Victorians certainly knew the Triangular hat that becomes a boat, the Paper dart, Fortune teller and a few others, and were introduced to more complex Japanese designs by a troupe of Japanese conjurors who toured Europe in the 1860s. In Spain, the traditional Pajarita (Sparrow), folded from a square, had been known for many years.

In Japan during the 1930s, a young engineer, Akira Yoshizawa, experimented with traditional designs and found that he could invent many designs of his own. His belief that origami was a creative art with boundless possibilities gained an increasing number of followers. Today origami is a respected creative art form in Japan. There are hundreds of books, dozens of creative designers, a number of regular periodicals and spectacular exhibitions of new work. Fittingly, Yoshizawa has been made a Living Treasure, the highest honour that Japan can give an artist, though he remains somewhat aloof.

In the West, a slow trickle of books or chapters in books appeared during the first half of this century, giving instructions for the simple folds that were then known. In the early 1950s a South African-born stage illusionist and magician resident in England, Robert Harbin, became very interested in paperfolding. His new creative work led to the first serious book to appear in the West, *Paper Magic*. The book inspired others to create, and established a network of creative paperfolders outside Japan. Contacts were soon made with Japan and the word 'origami' replaced 'paperfolding'. Further books by Harbin and the American Sam Randlett popularized the art and its new name. In 1967 the British Origami Society was formed, the first of ten or more societies now found outside Japan.

Today, origami has a wide appeal far removed from its old image as an inconsequential diversion for bored schoolboys. It is used in the media, taught in schools, employed as a therapy for people with damaged hands and is studied by mathematicians and designers. There are many books devoted to the subject and a growing number of courses. A few people even earn their living from origami.

What is its appeal? Most importantly, it is an art that anyone can do anywhere, anytime. All that is needed is a piece of paper and a pair of hands. What could be simpler? Therein lies the fascination of the art — making something beautiful or clever from a substance as everyday as paper, using no tools or machinery. The richness of the art comes from its purity.

# PAPER

**O**rigami paper would seem to be the natural choice for paper folding. However, it is not always possible to find packets of origami paper (the sheets of which are coloured on one side and white on the reverse), particularly if you live away from a large city. Japanese import shops usually sell it, as do good art and craft shops and the occasional toyshop, but it is not widely available. If you can find a shop that sells it then buy some, but it is better not to depend on it. In any case, origami paper is relatively expensive and has the unnerving ability to make almost everything folded with it look rather gaudy. Nevertheless, origami paper can sometimes be appropriate, particularly for geometric designs where strong colour is often important.

Instead, think of paper in two ways: paper for practice and paper for display. For practice, any cheap paper that will take a crease without cracking is ideal. The list could include typing paper, photocopy paper, computer paper, writing paper, brown wrapping paper and even pages cut from a magazine if nothing else is to hand. Avoid folding newspapers, paper towels, soft lavatory paper, tissues or paper used in duplicating machines. None of these papers holds a crease very well and they all crack or tear easily. Typing, photocopy and computer paper can be bought very cheaply in bulk from a printer and a batch will keep you in practice paper almost for ever. Use practice papers when you are unfamiliar with a design and want to understand how to make it.

The fun starts with choosing display papers! The introductory paragraphs to each design

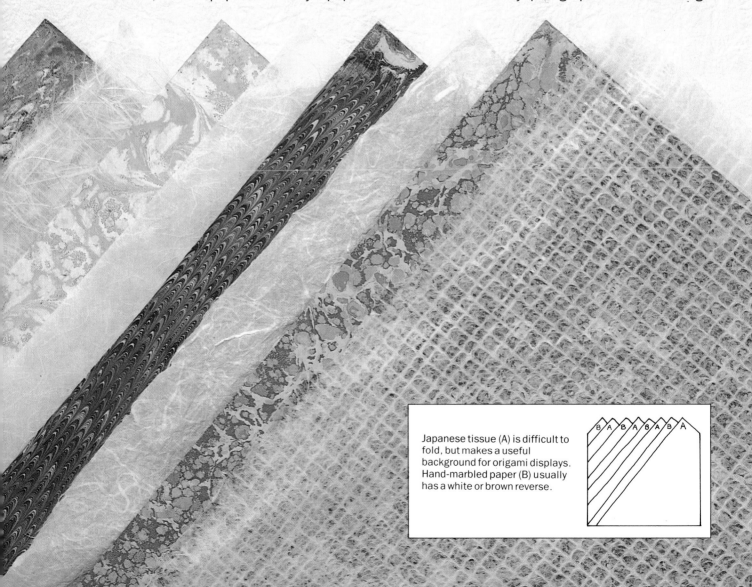

Japanese tissue (A) is difficult to fold, but makes a useful background for origami displays. Hand-marbled paper (B) usually has a white or brown reverse.

suggest papers to use and you should follow the advice, or you might fold with a paper that is too thin or too thick for that design. However, there is room for experimentation and you may wish to try papers other than those suggested.

The best place to look for these more exotic types of paper is in an art or craft shop. Large cities sometimes have shops which specialize in selling paper and these are definitely worth a visit. A good art or craft shop will stock a surprisingly wide range of papers. In particular, look for papers that have a textured or decorative surface. Other good papers include pastel paper, drawing paper, thin watercolour paper, coloured printing papers and any other paper that can hold a crease without cracking or tearing. Paper with a coloured coated surface that flakes off at the crease when folded is unsuitable. If you want a paper with a different colour on the two sides, buy gift-wrap paper from a stationery shop. Here you may also find paper-backed metallic foil, either by the sheet or in a long roll. Use it very sparingly, never for ani-

mals. Experiment also with hand-made paper, wallpaper, old posters and any other paper that looks interesting. However, avoid papers which are too beautiful or which have a very strident pattern on them – the folded design is overpowered by such papers, so that the eye takes in the paper, not the origami. Also, avoid folding card, papers coated on one side with a coloured pigment (poster paper) and papers with a shiny surface. They all crack.

Sometimes, the introductory paragraphs to the designs suggest that you use thin, medium or heavy (thick) paper. Paper weight is a complex subject, made doubly so because the United States has a system different to that of other countries, using pounds as opposed to grammes. So, to keep it simple; *thin* means paper such as airmail paper, undercopy (bank) typing paper or tissue; *medium* means any paper about as thick as a page in this book, or slightly thinner or thicker, but not by much; *thick* means any paper as thick as a glossy magazine cover.

Two-tone origami paper (C) has different colours on the front and reverse sides; decorative origami paper (D) has traditional Japanese patterns on one side and is white on the other side; and origami paper (E) is coloured on one side but white on the reverse.

Textured paper (F) is streaked and mottled; Ingres paper (G) is soft, flecked and best dampened before folding; metallic foil (H) is backed with white paper; patterned gift-wrap paper (I) is white on the reverse; and hand-made paper (J) is recognized by its rough, uncut edges. Use printing paper (K), manufactured for photocopy machines, to practise.

# GETTING STARTED

Before trying the various origami folds and projects, it pays to master
a few very basic techniques. The first of these is making a square.
Most of the designs in this book are folded from squares of paper but
few types of paper can be bought in this shape, so it helps to be able to
make a square accurately.
Next you can move on to the technique of folding. An origami design
will never look attractive if it has been folded badly — it is important to
learn how to move your hands correctly. And finally there is the origami
language itself — understanding how to follow the diagrams used in
this book, and indeed the vast majority of origami publications around
the world.

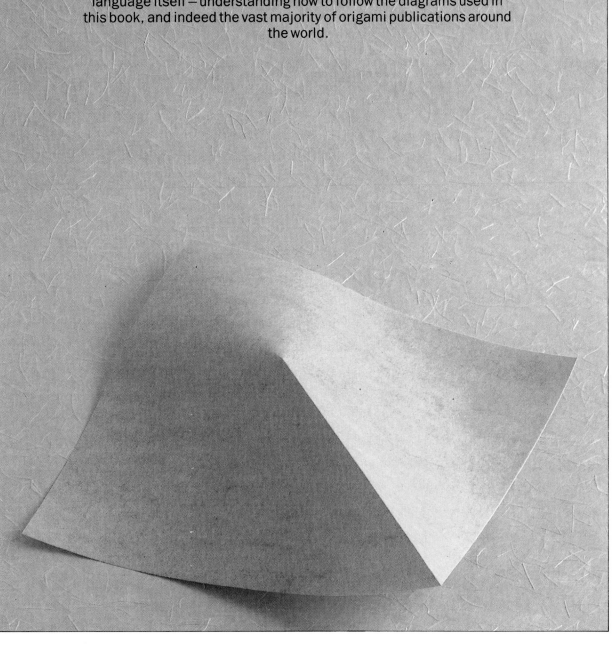

# HOW TO MAKE A SQUARE

Here are four methods that enable you to make a square from any oblong. Whichever you choose, trim off the excess paper with great care — nothing in origami is more frustrating than trying to fold a *nearly* square square! If the diagrams are a little confusing, check the symbols against the Table of symbols on pages 173–5.

## SIMPLE METHOD

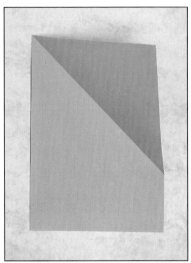

**1** Bring the top right-hand corner down to the left-hand side of the paper to form a triangle with an oblong strip beneath it . . .

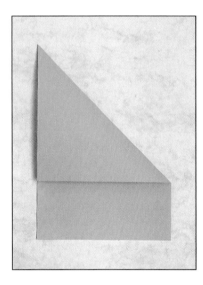

**2** . . . like this.

**3** Remove the oblong in one of the ways described below and open up the triangle . . .

**4** . . . to give a perfect square.

In Step 2 there are four basic ways to separate the triangle from the remainder of the paper beneath it:

**SCISSORS**
Use a large pair and cut very carefully along the bottom of the triangle.

**CRAFT KNIFE**
Lay one edge of a ruler along the bottom edge of the triangle and cut through the paper with a craft knife, pressing against the edge of the ruler. Make sure you place the paper on a suitable cutting surface, such as a sheet of thick card — or your best polished table might be sliced to shreds!

**NON-SERRATED KITCHEN KNIFE**
This is the neatest and quickest method. Make a fold across the bottom of the triangle. Lay the paper against a hard, level surface and slice along the length of the fold in a few bold strokes of the knife, with the blade up between the layers. This method may take a little practice, but is the best. A serrated knife will not cut the paper cleanly.

**TEARING**
Not recommended, but acceptable if none of the above methods are possible. For best results, bend the crease backwards and forwards several times before tearing, creasing very firmly each time. This will considerably weaken the paper and make tearing easier.

## NO-CREASE METHOD

The Simple method described above is very efficient, but leaves a diagonal crease on the paper which you may not want. There is an alternative, ingenious method that leaves the paper quite smooth.

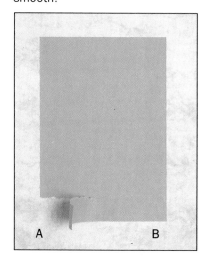

**1** Tear off the bottom edge AB.

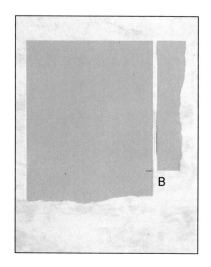

**2** Lay it against the side of the sheet and mark the sheet where it touches corner B.

**3** This is point X.

**4** Make a crease across the paper from X and trim off the lower portion using any of the suggestions in the Simple method.

**5** The square is uncreased.

## DAMAGED SHEET METHOD

Some large sheets of paper will have damaged edges, which means that the square has to be formed entirely within the sheet.

**1** Fold down the top edge.

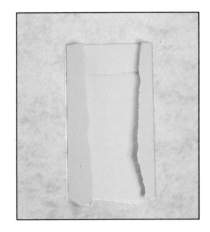

**2** Fold in the two side edges.

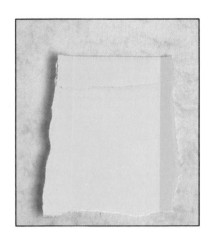

**3** Unfold.

**4** Trim off the excess, using any of the techniques suggested in the Simple method.

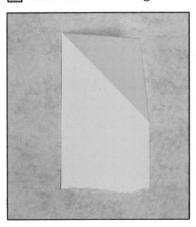

**5** Proceed to make a square as described in the Simple method.

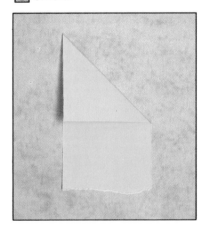

**6**

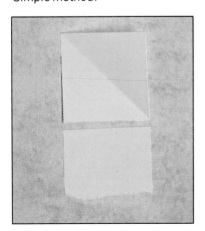

**7**

## GUILLOTINE METHOD

This is the easiest method because you don't need to cut the paper at all — somebody else does it for you!

The smart way to buy paper is not to get a thin packet of 20 sheets from a stationery shop, but to buy a ream (500 sheets) of photocopying or typing paper from a photocopy shop or small printer.

Buying these sorts of paper in bulk is much less expensive and the shop or printer will guillotine it perfectly square for a small additional sum. A ream costs about the same as five or six packets of 20 sheets.

# STARTING TO FOLD

Some people say they cannot use their hands. They believe that folding paper will be difficult and not pleasurable. This isn't true! Think of folding as a 'paper ballet' in which the hands move gracefully in large, controlled movements. Try not to let your fingers battle with the paper. Relax them. Let them move slowly and with deliberation. Paper is sensuous and yielding and responds to a caring touch, so do not let your hands move in an insensitive way.

People start to practise origami because they want to make flowers and gifts for friends, or for any number of other reasons. Few start because they want to enjoy the process of folding, almost regardless of the finished design. Most experts would agree, however, that with experience and the understanding that it brings, origami becomes a *folding* art, not a folded art. To quote the familiar phrase, 'it is better to travel than to arrive'. With this in mind, give a little time and thought to the process of folding.

For folding to give you pleasure, it is important not only that you know *how* to fold, but also that the sequence itself should be pleasurable. It should be direct, elegant, flowing and contain no irrelevant creases, bulky layers or clumsy techniques. A good design seems 'obvious' when it has been folded. Somehow it seems to have been in the paper all the time, waiting to be discovered, rather than created. By comparison, a poor design seems contrived, emerging from the paper only with some effort.

The quality of the sequences can be assessed when you come to fold the designs later in the book. This chapter starts by outlining some of the basic ways in which the paper should be handled. It is important to learn them – they will simplify folding for you and make it a pleasure.

Folding is often made simpler if you rest your paper on a hard, level surface, such as a table, drawing board or hard-backed book. Folding on a soft surface, such as on your lap or on a carpet, is not recommended. Having said that, experts like to fold everything in the air. Manipulating paper entirely within the hands is certainly very enjoyable, but it can also be very difficult. Nevertheless there will be times when, even as a beginner, you will need to pick up the paper to fold it, particularly towards the end of a design when you are putting in the smaller folds. These smaller folds are usually easy to make in the air, but the long, early folds which are a feature of most designs are more difficult. Here are some suggestions for how to crease them. Study the hand positions carefully and practise the exercises. Sit comfortably. These are the basic folds.

## CREASING A DIAGONAL

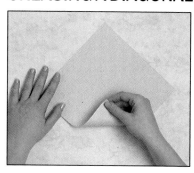

**1** Rest the paper on a hard, level surface so that a corner is pointing towards you. Pick up the corner and move it up to the top corner . . .

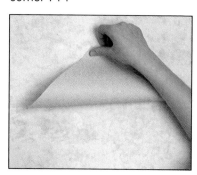

**2** . . . like this. Move it about until the two corners are exactly aligned. Don't rush!

**3** Hold the corners together with one hand. With the other, run the forefinger down the triangle, pressing hard. Continue . . .

**4** . . . to the bottom edge, then run the finger along to the right, making a crease.

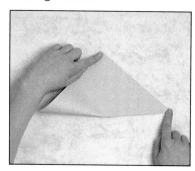

**5** Run the finger back along the bottom edge to the other corner . . .

**6** . . . completing the crease. Check that the top corners are still aligned.

## CREASING A BOOK FOLD

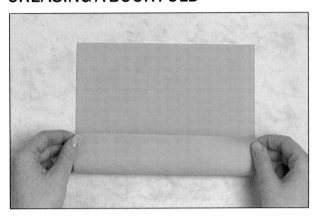

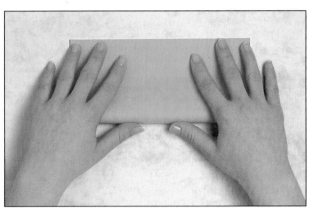

**1** A book fold is so called because it folds the paper in half to look like a book. Rest the paper on a hard, level surface so that an edge is near you. With a hand at each corner, lift up that edge and move it to the top edge . . .

**2** . . . like this. Hands on top, move the top layer to and fro until both the left and right corners are exactly aligned. Don't rush!

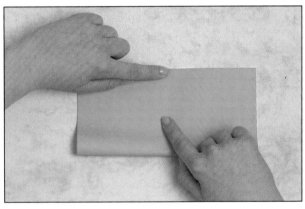

**3** With one hand, hold the top edges firmly together and slide the forefinger of the other firmly down the centre of the paper . . .

**4** . . . to the bottom edge. Run your finger along the bottom edge to the left and right . . .

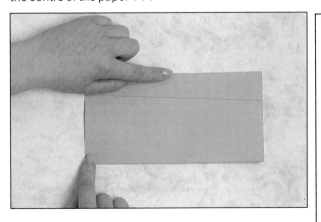

**5** . . . completing the crease. Check that the top corners are still aligned.

### TIPS

○ *Make a crease in one flowing sequence of hand movements, rather than a lot of stop-start, jerky ones. The crease will look better and you will enjoy the activity more.*

○ *Press each crease firmly.*

○ *Being able to make a good diagonal or book fold is very important. If they are made inaccurately, every other crease that follows will also be inaccurate. Take your time with these folds. Get them right.*

# THE HORIZONTAL-FOLD RULE

Always pick up the paper by the nearest edge or corner and *fold it away from your body*, making the crease across the bottom of the paper. This is quicker and more accurate than folding the paper from left to right, right to left or in any other direction.

To see for yourself, try folding diagonal creases by moving the paper in four different directions as shown here. The one labelled 'correct' should be the easiest.

correct

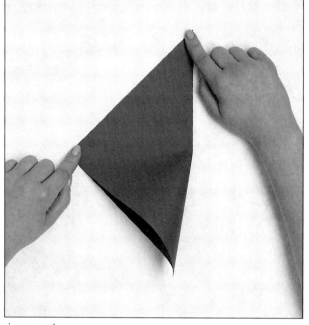

incorrect

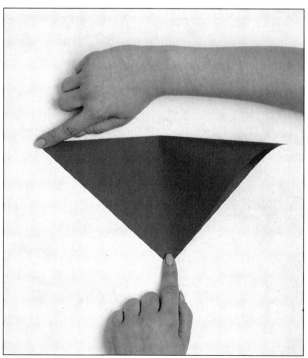

incorrect

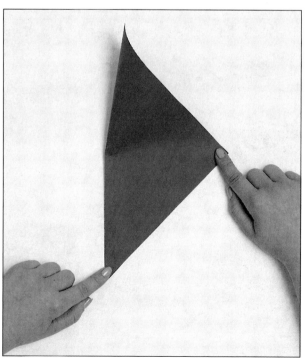

incorrect

The diagrams in the book will not always show a horizontal crease like this:

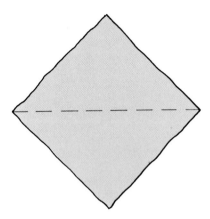

The crease might be shown vertically . . .

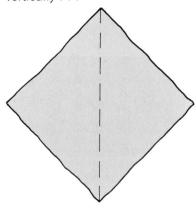

. . . or at an angle, like this .

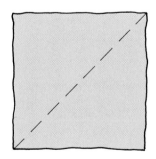

So the rule is: turn the paper around from one crease to the next so that you can always make the next crease horizontally across the bottom of the paper.

Practise the turning exercise shown below. Make the diagonal and book fold creases following the methods which were shown on pages 15–6.

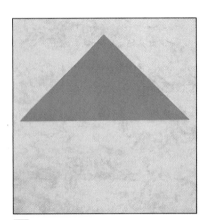

**1**

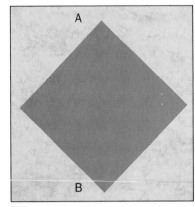

**2**

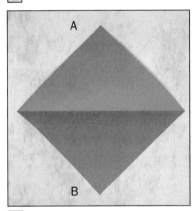

**3**

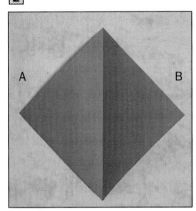

**4**

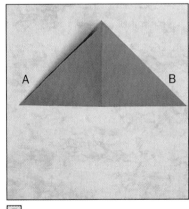

**5**

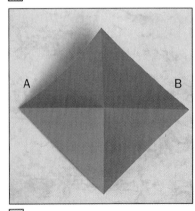

**6**

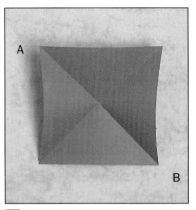

**7**

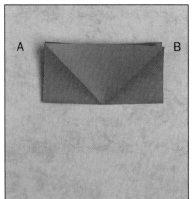

**8**

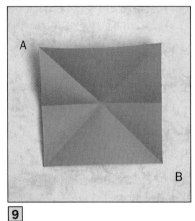

**9**

**10**

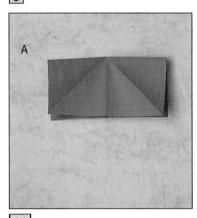

**11**

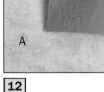

**12**

# FINAL CHECKS

Before starting to fold a design or designs, check that your preparations are correct.

### PAPER
Is the sheet the correct weight and size for your chosen design? Where it is important, the instructions will specify precisely what you need. If they do not, choose your own paper.

### SHAPE
Is the paper exactly square? If not, re-trim it.

### SURFACE
Is the surface you are folding on level and flat?

### FOLDING
Are you familiar with the correct ways to make the diagonal and book folds and do you know how to rotate the paper following the Horizontal fold rule?

### POSTURE
Are you sitting comfortably? This may seem a silly question, but a comfortable chair, a table at a good height and a straight back all help to make folding more enjoyable.

### ATTENTION
To get the most pleasure from folding, you must give it close attention. Gentle music in the background may not be distracting, but the television almost certainly will be. Turn it off.

ORIGAMI

ORIGAMI

# HOW TO FOLLOW THE DIAGRAMS

Diagrams are at the heart of a book about origami. No matter how simple a design, a confusing sequence of diagrams can make it unintelligible. What a good diagram must do is show a three-dimensional sheet of folding paper which is always moving, in a small number of two-dimensional, static diagrams.

During the last few decades, a system of terms and symbols has evolved which, as a result of much experimentation, has been shown to be both clear and concise. This system is now standard and is used in almost all good origami books. If you learn the symbols and techniques in this book you will be able to fold from almost any origami book in any language.

Each step in a diagram contains all the information you need to progress to the next one. If you become stuck, don't panic! Unfold the paper back to a point that you feel confident is correct. Refold from that point, paying very close attention to *all* the symbols and reading *all* the instructions. Have you perhaps folded two layers when it should have been one? Have you made a mountain when it should have been a reverse? Did you forget to turn the paper over? If you are still stuck, unfold the paper to a point even further back in the sequence: the most mystifying errors are often made near the start of a sequence.

This chapter introduces the basic diagrammatic conventions. When a new symbol is introduced, a few examples will be given to clarify its meaning. If you skip a few designs and come across an unfamiliar symbol which is not explained, turn to the Table of symbols at the back of the book (pages 173–5). Here the unfamiliar symbol will be listed with a page number showing where it first appeared and was explained.

# THE VALLEY FOLD

The fold is called a valley because, unfolded, the crease resembles a valley indented into the paper. Its symbol is a dashed line.

It is the simplest technique in origami and the most common. Often it is referred to simply as a fold or crease. So in this book you will read instructions such as 'fold A to B' rather than 'valley fold A to B. The word valley is only used when it is necessary to clarify whether a fold is a valley rather than a mountain. (A mountain, the opposite of a valley, is introduced in the next chapter.)

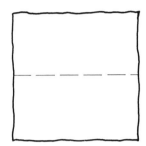

# THE ARROW

The valley fold symbol of dashed lines is often shown with an arrow to indicate the direction in which the paper moves when the fold is made (see below):
Fold the paper upwards (or downwards if the arrow points in the opposite direction).

Fold the paper to the right (or to the left if the arrow points in the opposite direction).

## THE LOOK-AHEAD RULE

When following a sequence of diagrams, before making a new fold it is often necessary to look ahead to the next diagram to see what the new folded shape looks like.

So, before making the fold in Step 1, it is helpful to look ahead to Step 2 to see what the shape of the paper will be after the fold has been made. Then look back to Step 1 and make the fold. The sequence may continue as follows:

Look at Step 4 before making the fold in Step 3. What shape are you trying to make?

Look at Step 6 before making the fold in Step 5. What shape are you trying to make?

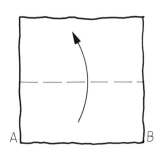

**1**

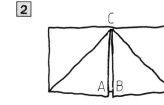

**2**

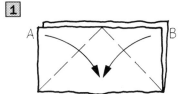

**3**

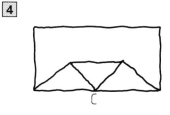

**4**

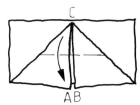

**5**

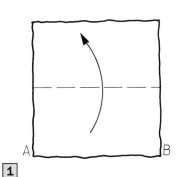

**6**

In the six diagrams above right, Steps 2 and 4 contain no symbols to move the sequence forward. To save space, these diagrams can be omitted, leaving just four diagrams.

Notice how Step 2 shows both the new shape of the paper after the Step 1 fold has been made, and contains the instructions for the new fold to make the Step 3 shape. Learn to look ahead.

**1**

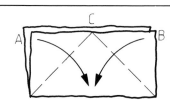

**2**

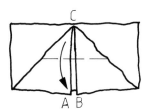

**3**

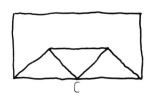

**4**

ORIGAMI

# PAPER DART
Make a Paper dart to familiarize yourself with the valley fold.

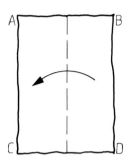

**1** Fold BD across to AC.

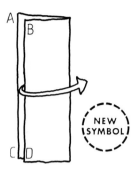

**2** Unfold.

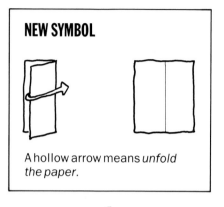
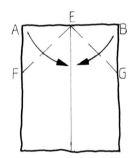

**3** Fold corners A & B to the centre crease, making a new corner at E.

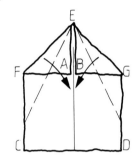

**4** Fold edges EF and EG to the centre crease, narrowing corner E.

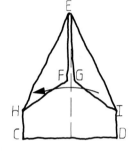

**5** Fold ID across to HC.

**6** Fold edge EI to EJ, folding corner E in half . . .

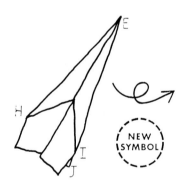

**7** . . . like this. Turn the paper over.

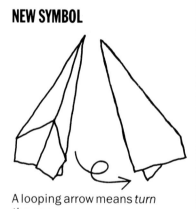
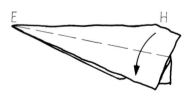

**8** Repeat on this side, folding EH to EJ.

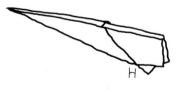

**9** Open the wings.

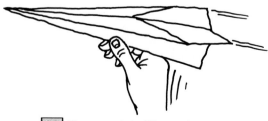

**10** The completed Paper dart. Balance the dart in your hand and throw gently.

# VALLEY/MOUNTAIN DESIGNS

The mountain fold is the opposite of the valley fold that was
introduced in the previous chapter. While a valley crease indents into
the paper, a mountain crease rises up like a mountain ridge.
A mountain fold is the same as a valley: the one is the other seen from
the reverse side of the sheet.

# BASIC EXAMPLE

This is the mountain fold symbol, a long dash followed by two dots:

Like the valley fold, it is often accompanied by an arrow to indicate the direction in which the paper moves when the fold is made. Note that the arrow is different from the valley fold arrow:

When a valley fold is being made, the part of the paper which moves during folding moves *to the front*, but when a mountain fold is being made, the part which moves, moves *behind*, see right.

A mountain fold is often awkward to make — bending the paper backwards is not easy. The trick is to turn the paper over and make a simple valley fold instead, then turn it back over to the front.

In the example (bottom right), try to imagine the extra steps that would be needed using only valley fold symbols, if Step 1 did not contain a mountain fold symbol.

Though fundamentally the same as a valley fold and awkward to do, the mountain fold is primarily used to reduce the number of diagrams needed to explain a sequence of folds.

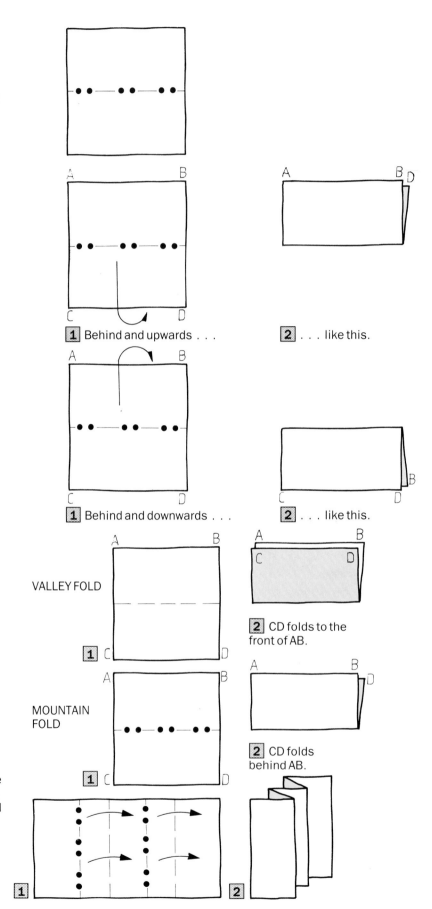

**1** Behind and upwards . . .    **2** . . . like this.

**1** Behind and downwards . . .    **2** . . . like this.

VALLEY FOLD

**2** CD folds to the front of AB.

MOUNTAIN FOLD

**2** CD folds behind AB.

# CHINESE GLIDER

This classic Chinese glider is one of a small number of similar simple gliders which have short bodies and wide wings. These characteristics make such a shape float gracefully and slowly through the air. Compare its stately performance with that of the sleeker Paper dart (see page 22). Use an oblong of strong, thin writing paper, typing paper or similar paper.

**TIP**

*Look carefully at all the steps. Follow the symbols and read all the captions.*

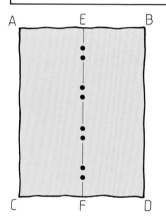

**1** Make a mountain crease down the middle (or make a valley fold, unfold, then *turn the paper over* so that it becomes a mountain crease).

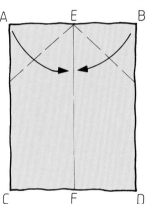

**2** Fold in corners A & B to the centre crease, making a corner at E.

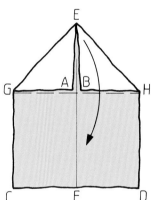

**3** Fold down E along GH.

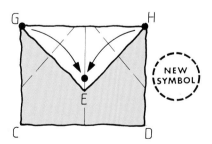

**4** Fold in G & H to a point a little above corner E. Do not fold it to E itself.

**NEW SYMBOL**

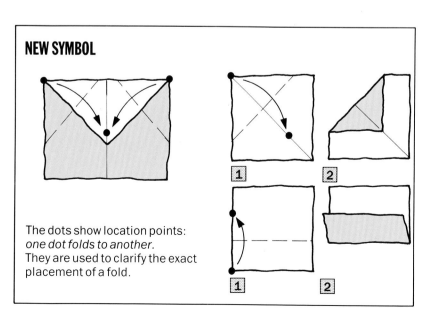

The dots show location points: *one dot folds to another.* They are used to clarify the exact placement of a fold.

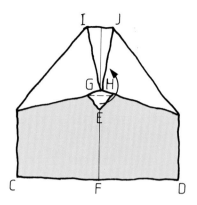

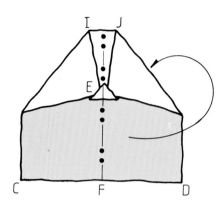

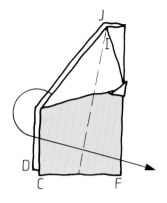

**5** Fold up E to lock G & H flat.

**6** Mountain fold in half. Note the direction of the arrow.

**7** From corner I, make a crease which slopes gently away from corner F. If you aren't sure exactly where the crease should go, draw a line on your paper copying the diagram, then fold along the line.

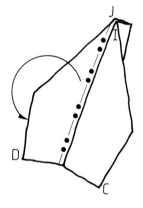

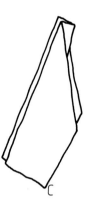

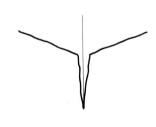

**8** Repeat behind with corner J. To form the crease, turn the paper over and make a valley fold.

**9** Open out the wings . . .

**10** . . . to this position.

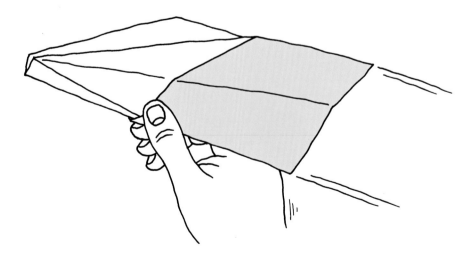

**11** The Chinese glider complete. Hold at the point of balance and throw level.

# MULTI BOX

Few origami designs are as adaptable as this simple traditional box. Though the sequence of steps will remain the same, the placement of some of the folds can be changed to produce an array of differently proportioned boxes, some sensible and practical, others very bizarre. Learn the Basic box, then experiment with some of the variations which follow. Use a square of strong paper, even paper-backed metallic foil.

## BASIC BOX

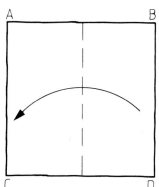

**1** Book fold in half.

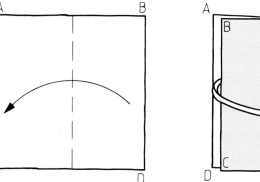

**2** Unfold.

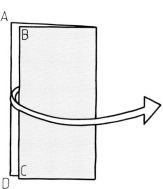

**3** Fold AC & BD to the centre crease.

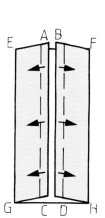

**4** Turn back edges AC & BD, to make two narrow hems identical in width. Look ahead to Step 5 to see what you are trying to fold.

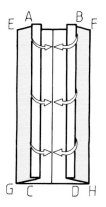

**5** Unfold Step 4.

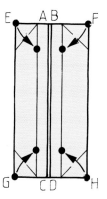

**6** Turn in corners EFG & H to touch Step 4 creases. Do not fold them into the middle.

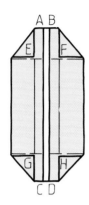

**7** Crease and unfold across the bottom of the EF triangles and across the top of the GH ones.

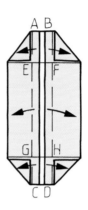

**8** Refold the hems on top of EG & FH.

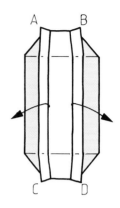

**9** Pull up AC & BD . . .

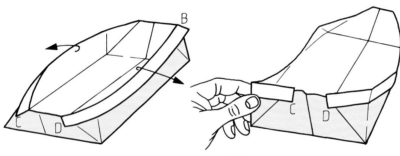

**10** . . . like this.

**11** Squeeze the corners to make them square.

**12** The Basic box complete.

## VARIATIONS ON THE BASIC BOX

The crease pattern of the Basic box can be summarized like this (see right).

Step 1 of the Basic box locates the centre crease. It does not matter whether this crease is horizontal or vertical because a square has four equal sides. However, if an oblong of paper is used, the direction of the centre crease does matter. The next two projects show how you can create different shaped boxes by altering the direction of the centre crease.

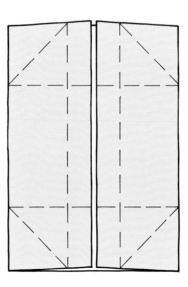

### TIP

*Make a few more basic boxes before trying the variations on the following pages. Fix the sequence in your mind so that you can fold from memory. This is easier than you might think.*

*Made from waterproof paper or kitchen foil, the box will hold liquids without leaking. Experiment, making the box in a variety of weights and sizes of paper, even dampened card.*

## LONG CREASE BOX

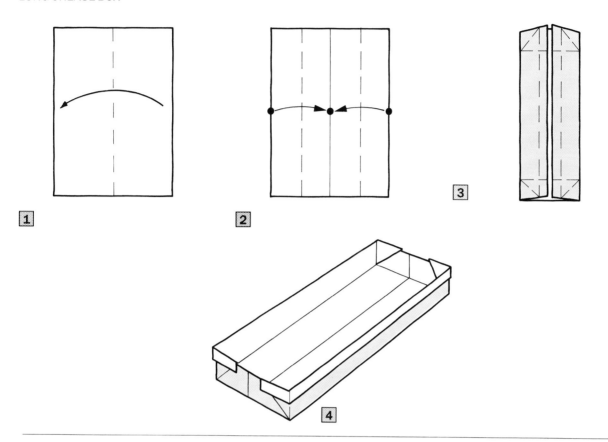

**1**  **2**  **3**

**4**

---

## SHORT CREASE BOX

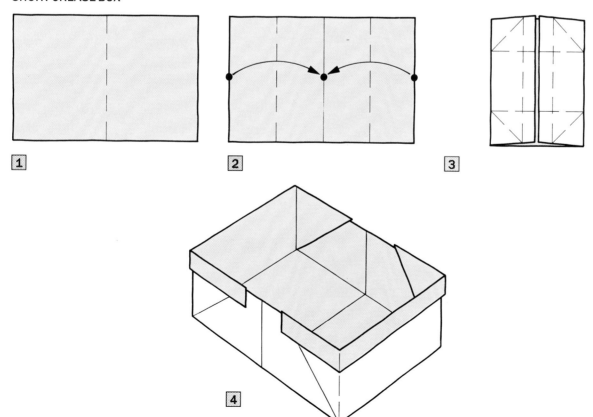

**1**  **2**  **3**

**4**

ORIGAMI

### SHALLOW BOX

In Step 3 of the Basic box, the edges are folded to the centre, but this need not be so. Here are three examples:

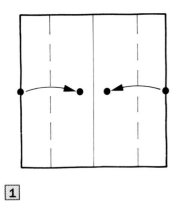

**1**

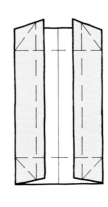

**2**

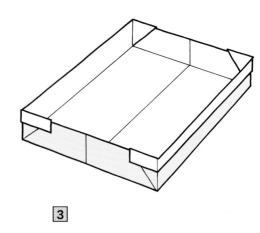

**3**

---

### DEEP BOX

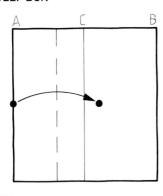

**1**

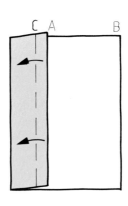

**2**

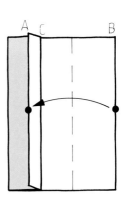

**3**

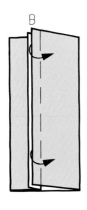

**4**

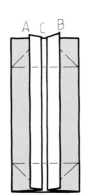

**5**

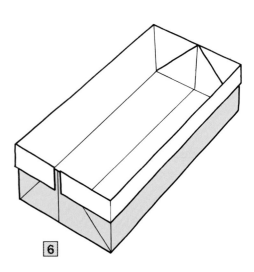

**6**

## LEANING BOX

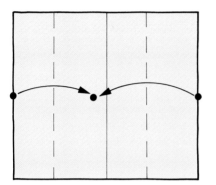

**1**

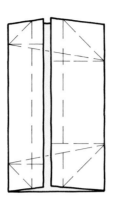

**2** The long sloping creases are made only on the underneath layer, not on the top.

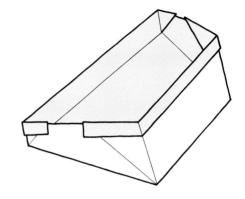

**3**

## DEEP HEMS
In Step 4 of the Basic box, the hems are folded back by a short distance, but this need not always be so. Here are three examples:

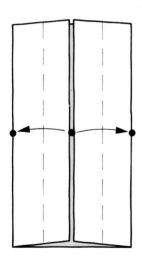

**1**

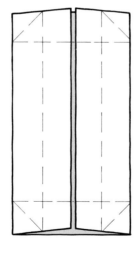

**2**

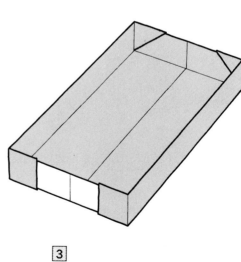

**3**

**ORIGAMI**

## BOX ON LEGS

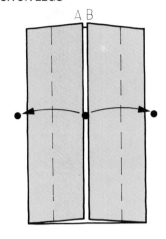

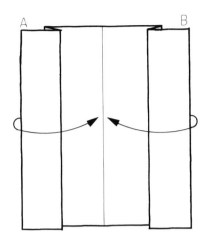

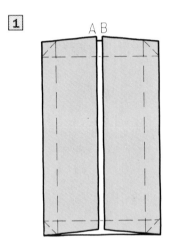

**1**

**3** Note how small the triangles look.

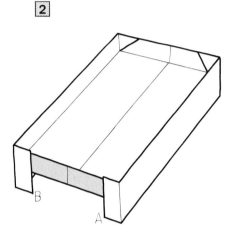

**2**

**4** If the 'legs' are weak, can you think of a way to strengthen them, perhaps by making them two layers thick?

## SLOPING BOX

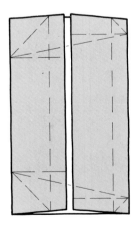

**1** The long sloping creases are made only on the underneath layer, not on the top.

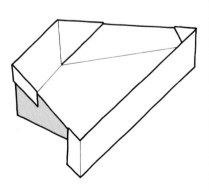

**2**

## CREATIVE SUGGESTIONS

○ Having seen that it is possible to move the folds on a square of paper, or to use an oblong of paper instead of a square, try to make other boxes by combining two of the above categories. For example, can you create a shallow box using the short crease of an oblong sheet, a leaning box with the long crease, or a tall box rather like a cereal packet? Experiment as broadly as possible. Don't just try to make sensible boxes, but see to what extremes you can push the Basic box, even to the point where it isn't a box at all! Perhaps also try turning it upside down to make a hat. What is the best shape for a tightly fitting hat? Square? Oblong? Deep? Can you make a box with a slightly larger lid? If so, is there a principle to follow so that the lid will always be a good fit over the box?

○ Origami is a truly creative art. By asking yourself interesting or awkward questions like those above, an ordinary design such as the Multi box can be transformed into an infinite variety of box-like shapes. The most intriguing results are often achieved when you set out to follow a theme, but do not know what the end result will look like. For example, what would happen if the four corners of the paper were not all right angles?

# SWAN

The Swan is a popular subject among creative paper-folders. This version is traditional and perhaps the simplest. Concentrate on making a neat point at the beak, so that the Swan retains its elegant shape. It is almost impossible to make a perfectly neat point – the paper is too thick and the spike too sharp – but take your time in making it as neat as possible. Use a square of good quality white paper, not too thick, for best results.

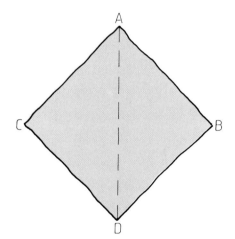

**1** Crease and unfold a diagonal.

**2** Bring edges AC & AB in to the centre crease . . .

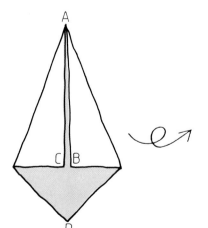

**3** . . . like this. Turn over.

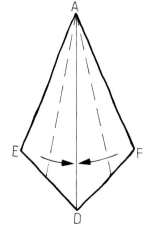

**4** Bring edges AE & AF in to the diagonal crease. Keep A as sharp as possible.

**5** Fold A down to D.

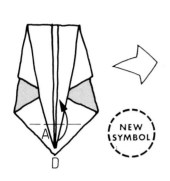

**6** Fold back A a little way. (The next drawing is bigger.)

## NEW SYMBOL

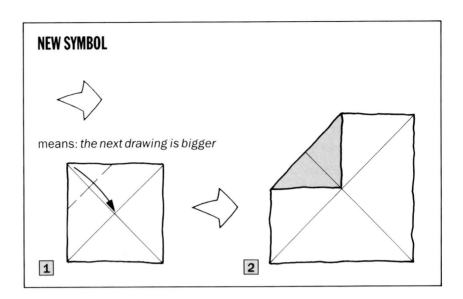

means: *the next drawing is bigger*

1

2

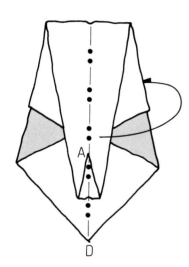

**7** Mountain fold in half through all layers . . .

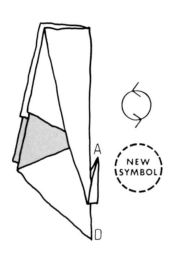

**8** . . . like this. Rotate the paper to look like Step 9.

## NEW SYMBOL

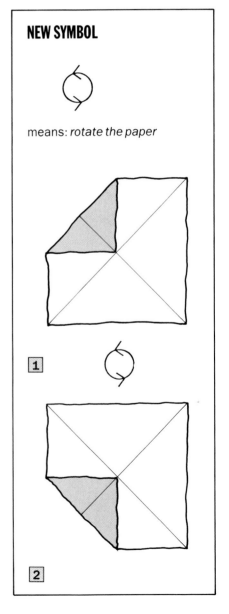

means: *rotate the paper*

1

2

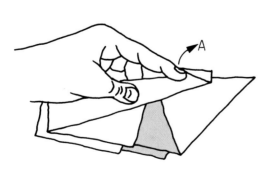

**9** Lift up the beak with a finger, then . . .

ORIGAMI

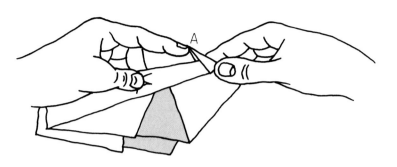

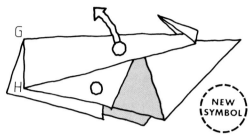

**10** . . . squeeze the top of the head flat to make a new crease. The head will stay away from the neck.

**11** Similarly, hold the bottom of the paper with one hand and with the other lift up the neck . . .

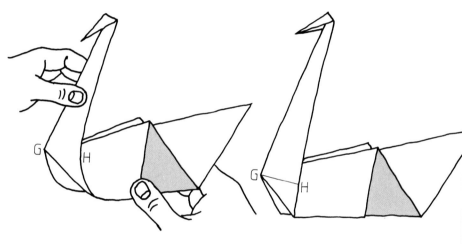

**12** . . . like this. Squeeze the bottom of the neck flat near GH to keep the neck in an upright position.

**13** The Swan complete.

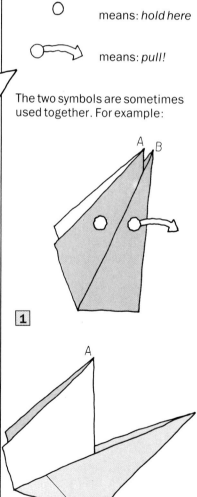

### NEW SYMBOL

○　　　means: *hold here*

means: *pull!*

The two symbols are sometimes used together. For example:

**1**

**2**

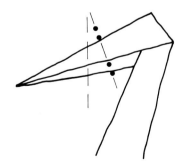

**14** A variation is to open out the head and make a mountain/valley pleat as shown, to create a separate beak . . .

**15** . . . like this. This is not particularly easy, but worth trying.

# CHRISTMAS DECORATION

Many geometric designs can be made from two or more identical units. In origami this is known as 'Modular folding'. Purists argue that using more than one sheet is, strictly speaking, not origami but a form of collage and that anything made from a number of sheets can also be made from a single sheet. Many enthusiasts would disagree with this narrow definition of origami and in recent years some remarkable modular systems have been created. Some systems are very complex, but the one here is quite simple. The knack of locking the two modules together is in Step 8 and is not immediately obvious since it relies on tensions, not flaps being tucked into pockets, as is usual in modular origami. Use two pieces of different coloured paper about 10 cm (4 in) square. This is one of my own designs.

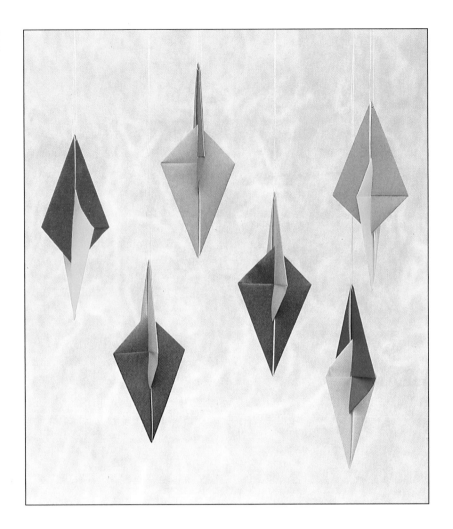

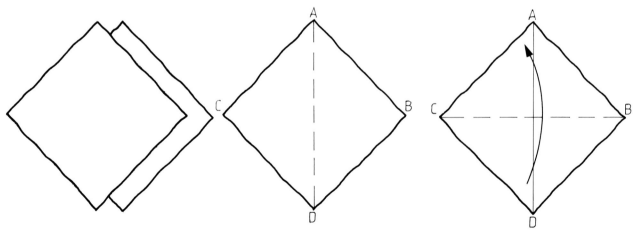

**1** Begin with two squares as described above.

**2** Crease and unfold the vertical diagonal.

**3** Fold the other diagonal. Leave it folded.

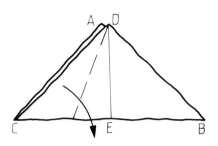

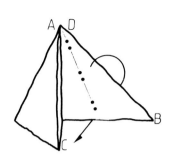

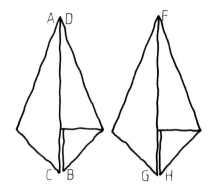

**4** Folding both layers together, start a valley crease at corner AD so that edge ADC is brought to lie along crease ADE . . .

**5** . . . like this. Similarly, mountain fold edge ADB behind (or turn the paper over and make a valley fold).

**6** The completed module. Make another. Check that C & B and G & H are neatly butted together — this is important if the modules are to interlock strongly.

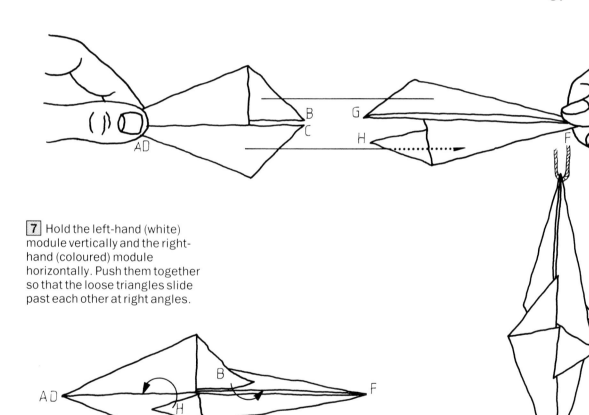

**7** Hold the left-hand (white) module vertically and the right-hand (coloured) module horizontally. Push them together so that the loose triangles slide past each other at right angles.

**8** Now the important part! The decoration will not lock unless the four triangles B, C, G and H are *all* correctly positioned. Push corner H upwards so that it rests on top of edge ADB and pushes back down against it. Similarly push B forwards to lie in front of edge HF.

Repeat behind with G & C, locking the corners behind the edges. Make sure the modules are kept at right angles to each other. When all triangles are locked in position, the decoration will hold a stable cross shape under tension.

**9** The Christmas decoration complete. Suspend by a thread from one corner.

# FAN

This practical design is included as an exercise in careful folding. Make each crease very precisely, taking your time. Properly done, Step 11 should be a neat row of equal pleats. In Steps 4–11, look closely at the dots and decide which edge is to be folded to which crease before making a fold, as a mistake at this stage may confuse you later. Use an oblong of paper, any size between 20 × 30 cm (8 × 12 in) and 30 × 45 cm (12 × 18 in). The paper should be thin or of medium weight and will look very attractive patterned or decorated. I adapted this design from the traditional fan.

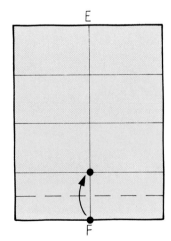

**1** Fold edge AC across to BD, making crease EF. Unfold.

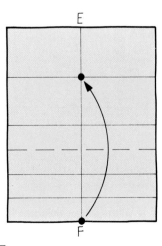

**2** Fold F up to E. Unfold.

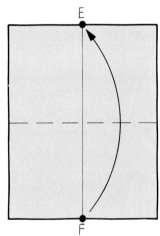

**3** Fold E and F in to the centre crease. Unfold both.

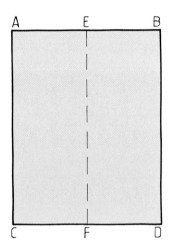

**4** Fold F up to the quarter crease. Unfold, then . . .

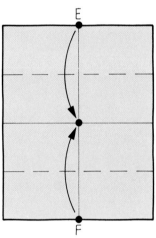

**5** . . . fold F up to the three-quarter crease. Unfold.

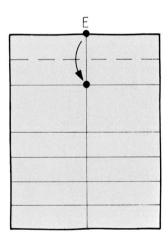

**6** Similarly, fold E down to the quarter crease. Unfold, then . . .

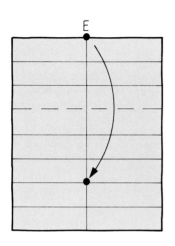

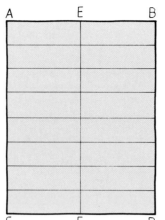

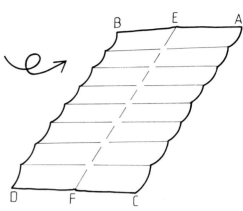

**ORIGAMI**

**7** . . . fold E down to the three-quarter crease. Unfold.

**8** This is the crease pattern. The paper is divided into eight equal divisions, all valley creases. Turn over . . .

**9** . . . so that the creases are all mountains.

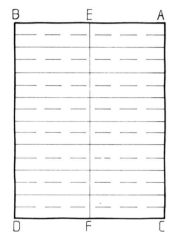

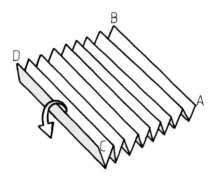

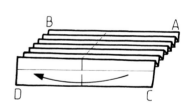

**10** Carefully place valley folds midway between each mountain, so that the paper pleats . . .

**11** . . . like this. Pull down edge CD, unfolding the first valley.

**12** Fold in half.

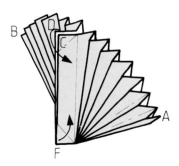

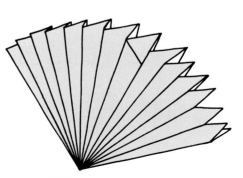

**13** Fold in F. Fold in the double layer corner DC, locking together the two halves of the pleats.

**14** Tuck the loose pleat right in to the line of pleats.

**15** The Fan complete.

# BACK-TO-FRONT SERVIETTE

Serviette-folding goes back several centuries to an age when European court banquets were often decorated with very elaborate pleated and starched fabric designs, some representing animals. Since scant documentation of these designs has survived, we unfortunately do not know how they were made. Serviette-folding was reinvented in the nineteenth century by cooks and restaurateurs and today perhaps a hundred designs are known. The design shown here is one of the lesser known folds. Like all serviette folds it holds its shape better when made from thick 3-ply paper serviettes, rather than the thinner 1- or 2-ply ones. The key to the design is at Step 6 — look carefully at the lettered corners and check Step 7 to see how the shape transforms.

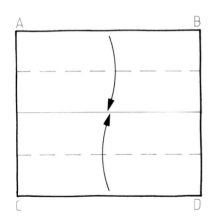

**1** An opened paper serviette will already have a centre crease. Fold edges AB and CD to that crease . . .

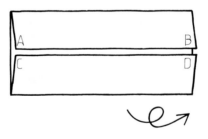

**2** . . . like this. Turn over.

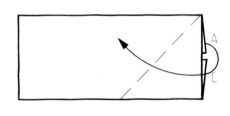

**3** Fold up the bottom right-hand corner, taking C and A with the crease.

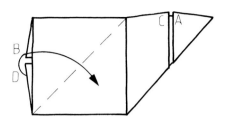

**4** Similarly, fold down the top left-hand corner, taking B and D with the crease . . .

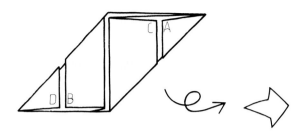

**5** . . . like this. Take careful note of A, B, C, and D. Turn over. (The next drawing is bigger.)

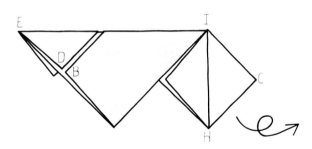

**6** Fold edge EH up to GF, but allow corner G to swivel downwards. Look at Step 7 to see where the lettered corners are.

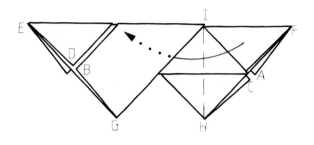

**7** Tuck F under corner G by creasing from I to H. Leave corner C at the right. Look ahead!

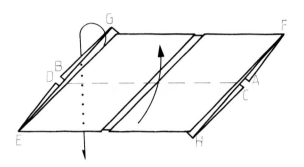

**8** This is the new shape. Turn over.

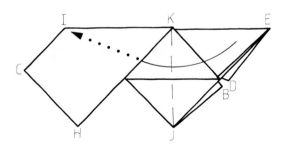

**9** Similarly, tuck E under corner H, by creasing from K to J. Leave corner B at the right.

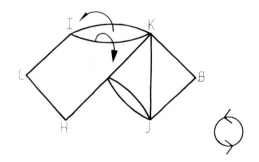

**10** Pull open the pocket between I and K. Turn the design upside down.

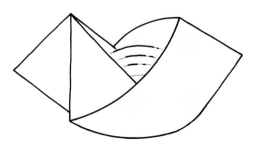

**11** The Back-to-front serviette complete.

# LETTERFOLD

Many letterfolds and envelopes have been developed in origami, perhaps because it is an intriguing technical challenge to try to create pockets into which loose flaps can be tucked. Some designs are too fussy, others rather dull, but the one shown here is simple and wonderfully elegant. Use an oblong sheet of writing paper. A picture of the Letterfold appears on page 1.

THE DESIGN IS TRADITIONAL

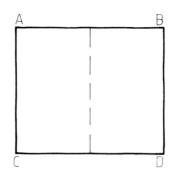

**1** Fold edge AC across to BD. Unfold.

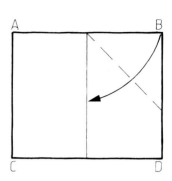

**2** Fold in corner B to lie along the centre crease.

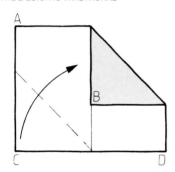

**3** Similarly, fold in corner C.

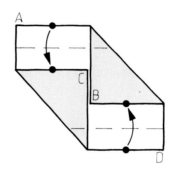

**4** Fold one dot on to the other, top left and bottom right.

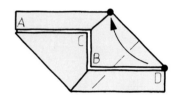

**5** Fold the dot at D on to the other . . .

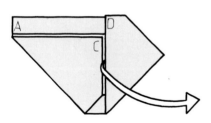

**6** . . . like this. Unfold.

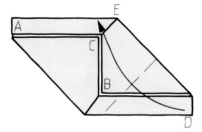

**7** Refold Step 5, but tuck D under corner E.

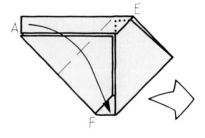

**8** Repeat Steps 5 to 7 with corner A, tucking it under F. (The next drawing is bigger.)

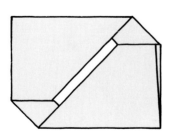

**9** The Letterfold complete.

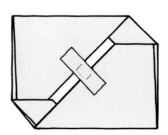

**10** For extra safety, place a piece of adhesive tape across the middle.

**CREATIVE SUGGESTION**
*Some paper-folders send their mail using this letterfold . . . so could you. Write your letter on the inside of the paper, fold it up and use a printed name and address sticker to hold the edges together, as suggested in Step 10. Write the recipient's name and address on the other side and stick on a stamp. Voilà!*

ORIGAMI

# FLYING EAGLE

Carefully made, this design will float a surprisingly long way. It does not, of course, look quite like a real eagle, but its slow glide captures the grace of the bird. Experiment with different ways of holding the design for launch, altering the speed at which it is pushed and the angle of release, as they will all affect its performance. Use a sheet of thin paper, between 10 cm (4 in) and 20 cm (8 in) square.

DESIGN BY JOHN SMITH (ENGLAND)

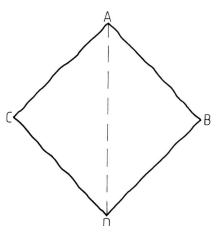

**1** Crease the vertical diagonal. Unfold.

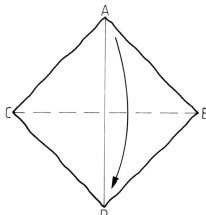

**2** Fold A down to D.

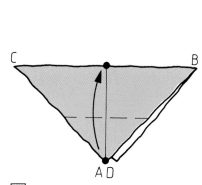

**3** Fold AD up to the top edge.

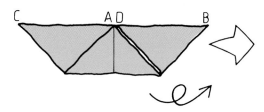

**4** Turn over. (The next drawing is bigger.)

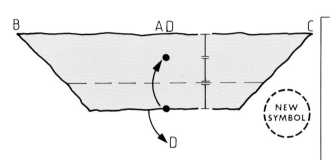

**5** Fold the bottom edge to a point two-thirds of the way up the central crease. Allow AD to flip downwards. Look at Step 6.

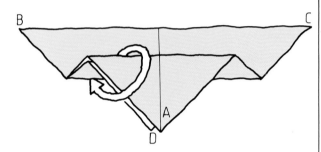

**6** Refold to Step 5, unfolding the Step 5 crease.

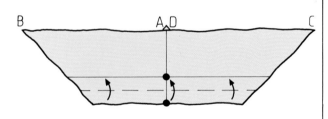

**7** Fold the bottom edge up to the Step 5 crease.

## NEW SYMBOL

means: *these distances are equal*

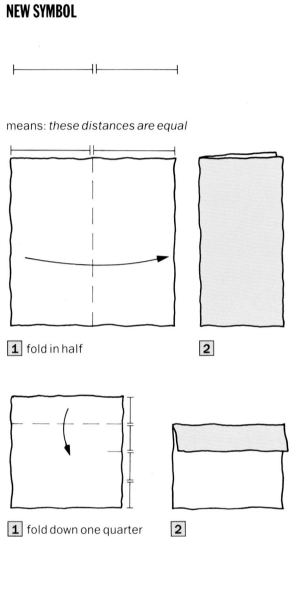

**1** fold in half

**2**

**1** fold down one quarter

**2**

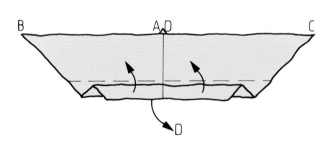

**8** Refold the Step 5 crease, allowing AD to flip down again.

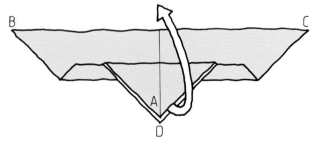

**9** Unfold corner A, lifting it right away from D.

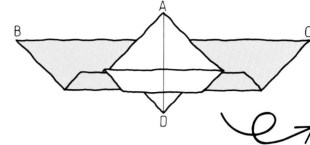

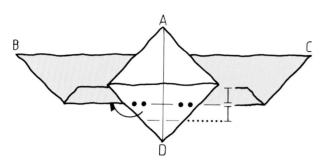

**10** Pleat D to be the same width as the thick band behind it . . .

**11** . . . like this. Turn over.

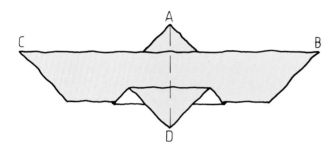

**12** Valley fold down the middle . . .

**13** . . . to give this angle when seen from the front.

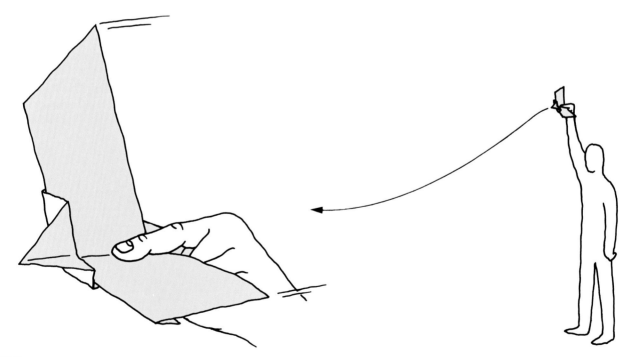

**14** The Flying eagle complete. Hold as shown.

**15** Hold the bird high above your head and release it with a gentle push rather than a throwing action.

ORIGAMI

# PISTOL

Few origami designs include rolling and bending — most are made only from straight creases. This unusual traditional pistol also has a unique lock which holds the handle to the barrels, more akin to macramé (string knotting) than origami. Use two sheets of writing paper, or a similar paper such as typing paper or photocopy paper, about 20 × 30 cm (8 × 12 in). Start with two identical oblongs.

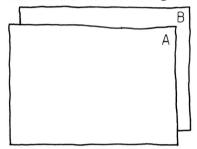

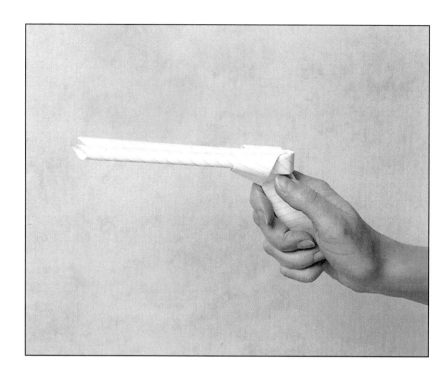

**HANDLE**

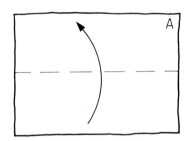

**1** Fold one oblong in half, bringing the long edges together. Then . . .

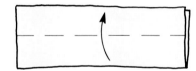

**2** . . . fold in half again . . .

**3** . . . and again!

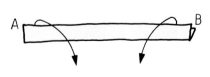

**4** Bend A & B to the front, rather like a shirt collar.

**5** Bend in the outer faces of the collar marked X, so that the two X's touch . . .

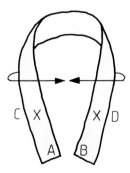

**6** . . . like this.

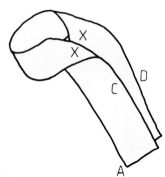

**BARRELS**

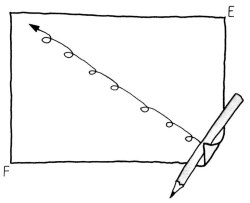

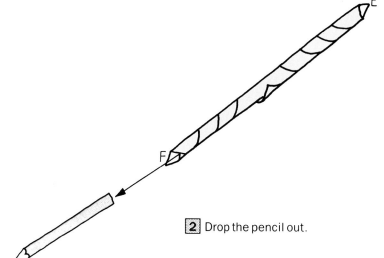

**1** With the other oblong, lay a pencil across a corner, and roll it to the opposite corner to form a tube, taking the pencil with it.

**2** Drop the pencil out.

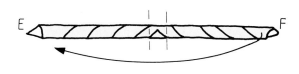

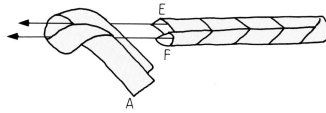

**3** Fold in half. This will stop the tube unrolling.

**4** Feed barrel F through the front twist in the handle and E through the rear twist . . .

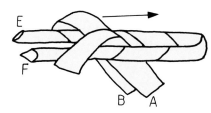

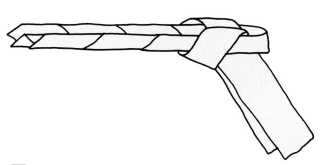

**5** . . . like this. Push the barrels through the handle as far as they will go.

**6** The Pistol complete.

# JAPANESE BOX

Boxes abound in origami! Most are basic, straight-sided boxes like the Multi box (pages 27–32) held together by an ingenious lock, but this box is more decorative than most. Use a square of strong paper or paper-backed metallic foil about 20 cm (8 in) square. I designed this box with a shape the same as a traditional Japanese box made from a 3 × 2 oblong. It is folded by a completely different method, however, and is an adaptation of a traditional design for a crown hat.

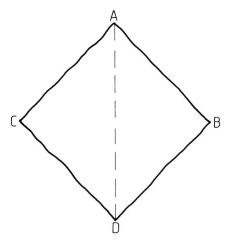

**1** Crease a diagonal. Unfold.

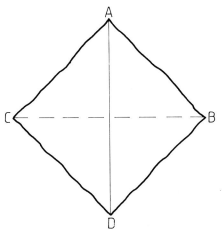

**2** Crease the other diagonal. Unfold.

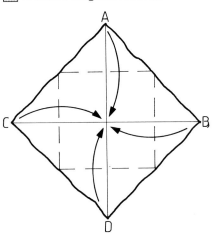

**3** Fold all the corners to the centre . . .

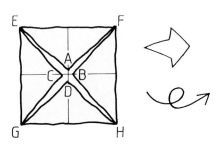

**4** . . . like this. Turn the paper over. (The next drawing is bigger.)

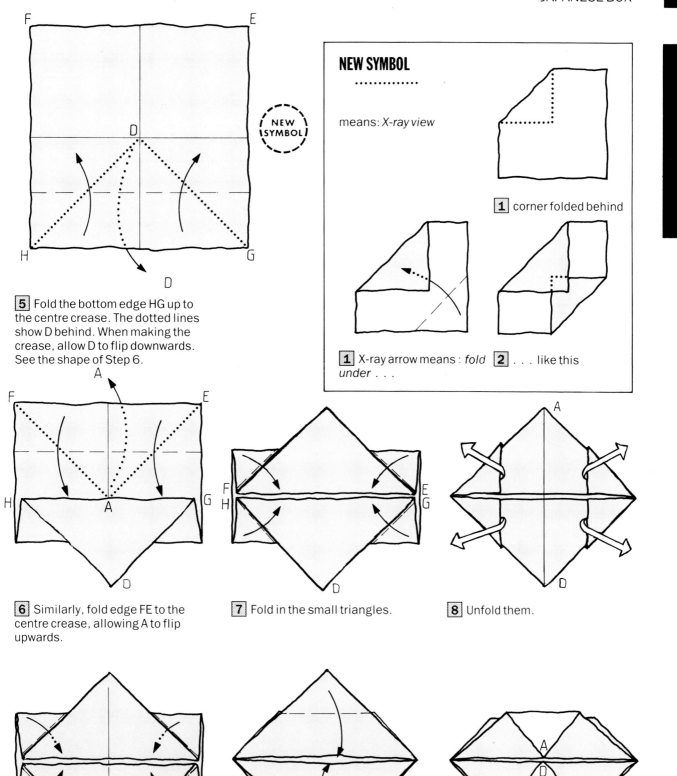

**NEW SYMBOL**

················

means: *X-ray view*

**1** corner folded behind

**1** X-ray arrow means : *fold under . . .* **2** *. . . like this*

**5** Fold the bottom edge HG up to the centre crease. The dotted lines show D behind. When making the crease, allow D to flip downwards. See the shape of Step 6.

**6** Similarly, fold edge FE to the centre crease, allowing A to flip upwards.

**7** Fold in the small triangles.

**8** Unfold them.

**9** Refold, tucking the small triangles underneath the big triangles.

**10** Fold A & D to the centre.

**11** Turn over.

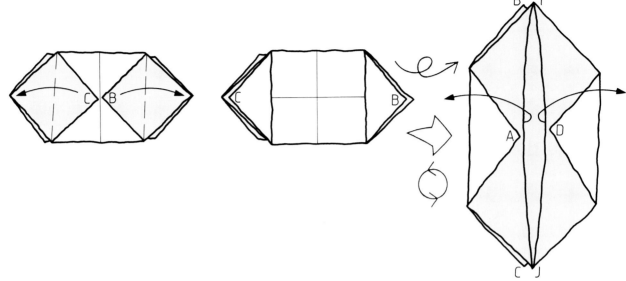

**12** Fold corners C & B to the outside . . .

**13** . . . like this. Turn the paper over. Rotate it. (The next drawing is bigger.)

**14** Open the pocket beneath AD . . .

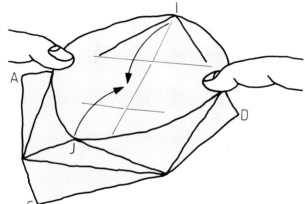

**15** . . . pulling it with a finger at each side. As the pocket becomes wider and wider, I & J start to come together . . .

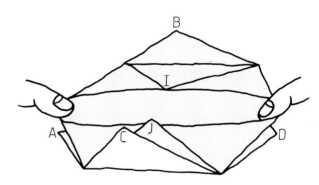

**16** . . . like this. Take your fingers out of the pockets and flatten the paper with sharp creases . . .

**17** . . . like this. Note that I & J are now touching and that A & D have separated. Compare the shape of the paper with Step 14.

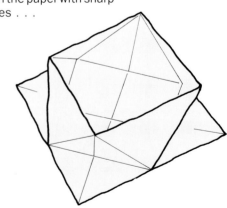

**18** Open the pocket to a shape midway between Steps 14 and 17. The Japanese box complete.

# ROBOT

Don't be discouraged from making this design just because it has a great number of steps. All the folds are easy to make and the result is definitely worthwhile. Keep a careful note of where you are in a sequence. Watch the lettered corners. Use three squares of medium-weight paper. The body and legs are made from identical squares, the head from a square whose side is half as long as the other squares. For example, the body and leg squares could be 20 cm (8 in) and the head square 10 cm (4 in).

Design by Yoshihisa Kimura (Japan).

**BODY AND ARMS**

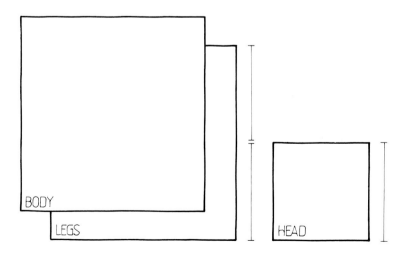

Begin with three squares as described above.

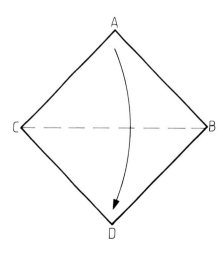

**1** Take one square and fold A down to D.

**ORIGAMI**

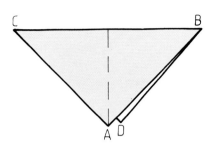

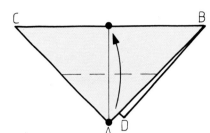

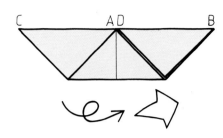

**2** Fold C across to B. Unfold.

**3** Fold AD to the top edge.

**4** Turn the paper over.

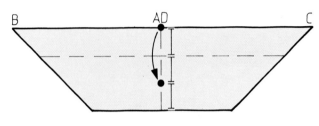

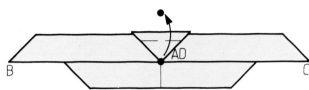

**5** Fold edge BC to a point two-thirds of the way down the crease. Bring AD with it.

**6** Fold AD back up as shown.

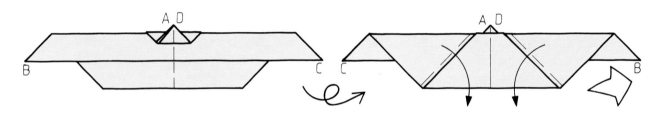

**7** Turn the paper over.

**8** Fold down C & B. (The next drawing is bigger.)

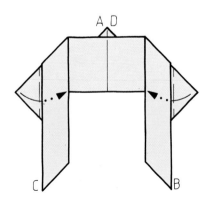

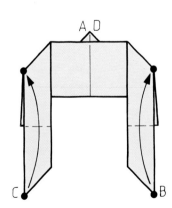

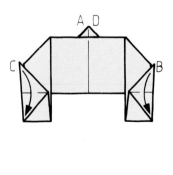

**9** Tuck the triangles inside.

**10** Fold up C & B as shown . . .

**11** . . . and down again.

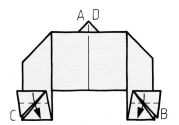

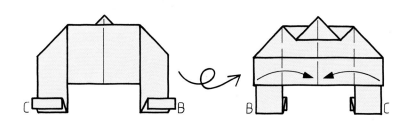

**13** Arms complete. Turn the paper over.

**14** Fold the sides to the middle.

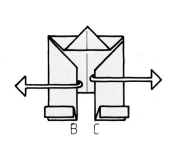

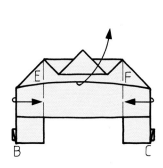

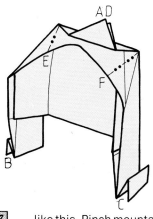

**15** Unfold.

**16** Refold Step 14, but lift the long edge EF to make a three-dimensional shape . . .

**17** . . . like this. Pinch mountain creases at E & F to square the shoulders like the corners of a box . . .

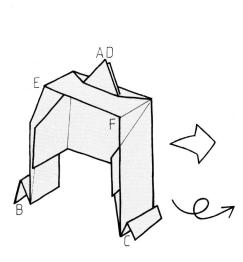

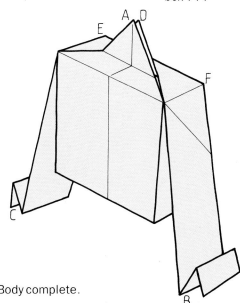

**18** . . . like this. Turn paper over.

**19** The Body complete.

**LEGS**

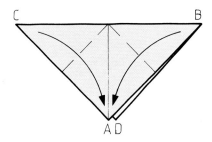

**1** Using the second square, begin with Step 1 of the body. Fold C & B down to corner AD.

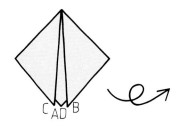

**2** Turn the paper over.

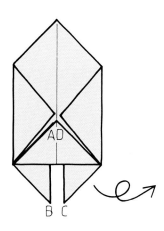

**3** Fold AD to the top corner, but pinch only at the centre to locate the middle of the shape.

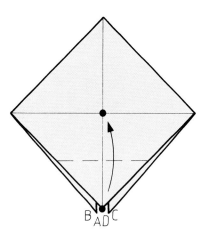

**4** Fold AD to the centre.

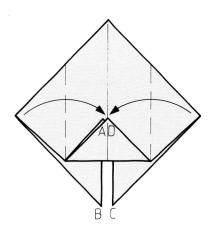

**5** Fold the left and right corners to the centre.

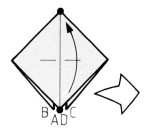

**6** Turn the paper over.

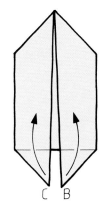

**7** Fold up C & B as shown . . .

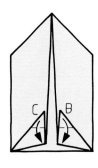

**8** . . . then back down . . .

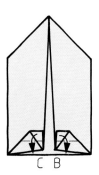

**9** . . . and in half.

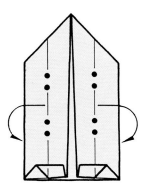

**10** Mountain fold the vertical edges behind at 90° . . .

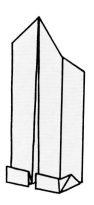

**11** . . . so that the completed Legs can stand.

## HEAD

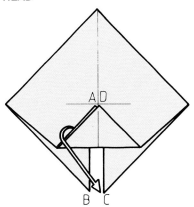

**1** Using the third, smallest, square, begin with Step 3 of the Legs. Unfold AD.

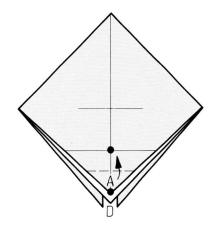

**2** Fold single layer A to the crease just unfolded. Do not touch D.

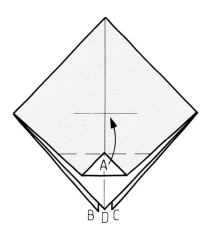

**3** Fold up along the unfolded crease.

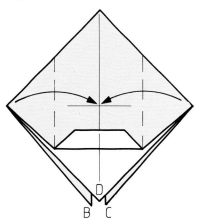

**4** Fold the left and right corners to the centre . . .

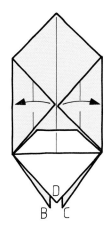

**5** . . . then fold the corners back out to the edge.

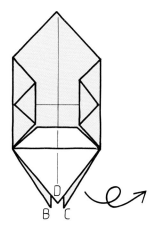

**6** Turn the paper over.

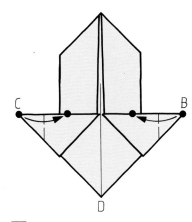

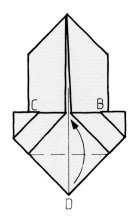

**7** Fold out C & B as shown.

**8** Fold in C & B, folding one dot on to the other, as shown.

**9** Fold up D to the centre.

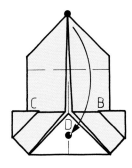

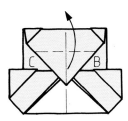

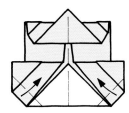

**10** Fold down the top corner as shown, to a point a little below D.

**11** Fold the corner back up, as shown.

**12** Turn in the bottom corners.

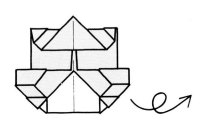

**ASSEMBLY**

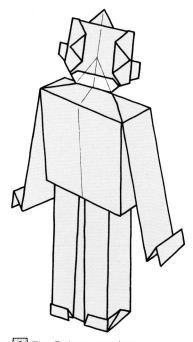

**13** The back of the Head should look like this. Turn it over.

**1** Tuck the point on the top of the Body up between the layers at the bottom of the Head. Balance the Body on the Legs. It might help to glue them together.

**2** The Robot complete.

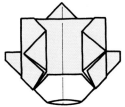

**14** The Head complete.

# SANTA CLAUS

This charming design makes full use of both sides of the paper to create a contrast between the red costume and the white face and edging. Many designs use this two-colour effect, such as the False nose and moustache (pages 82–3) and the Bugatti (pages 125–30). Use two identical squares of thin paper, red on one side and white on the other. If such paper is not available, fold a red sheet and white sheet back-to-back.

DESIGN BY YOSHIHIDE MOMOTANI (JAPAN).

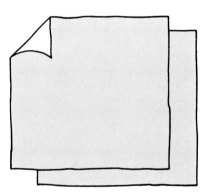

**HEAD AND BODY**

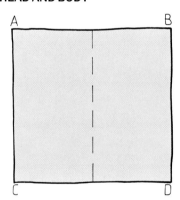

**1** Red side up, make a vertical valley crease down the middle. Unfold.

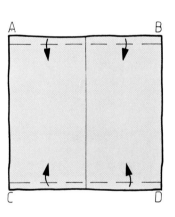

**2** Fold in edges AB & CD by a very small amount.

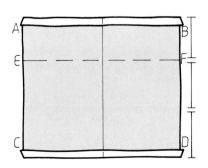

**3** Make crease EF one-third of the way down the paper from edge AB. Unfold.

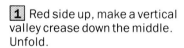
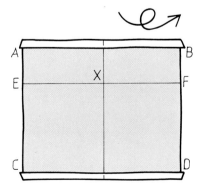

**4** Note point X. Turn the paper over.

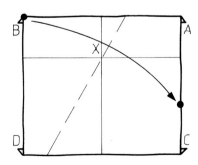

**5** Fold B to edge AC, so that the crease *passes through* point X.

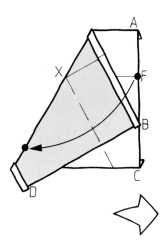

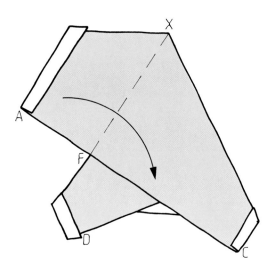

**6** Similarly, fold F across to the edge below X, so that the crease *runs into* X. (The next drawing is bigger.)

**7** Fold A across.

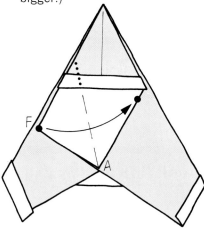

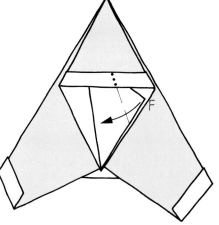

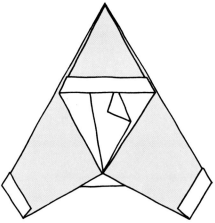

**8** Fold dot to dot. Note that the top of the crease disappears beneath the hood.

**9** Fold F back across to create a nose.

**10** The Head and Body complete.

**LEGS**

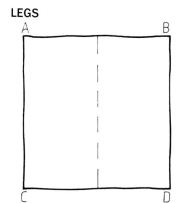

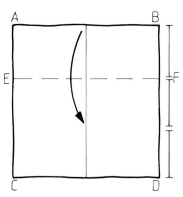

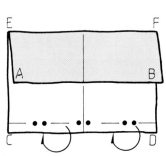

**1** White side up, make a vertical valley crease down the middle. Unfold.

**2** Make crease EF one-third of the way down the paper from edge AB. Keep it folded.

**3** Mountain fold edge CD behind, in the same place as the creases made in Step 2 of the Head and Body.

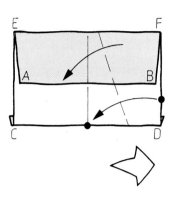

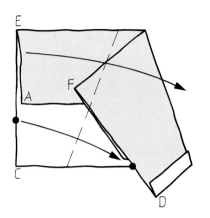

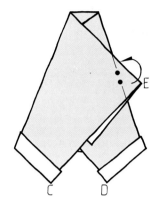

**4** Fold dot to dot.

**5** Again, fold dot to dot.

**6** Tuck E behind.

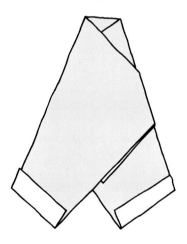

**7** The Legs complete.

**CREATIVE SUGGESTION**

*The two halves of the design can be brought together in a variety of lively positions. Make a frieze of different Santas.*

**ASSEMBLY**

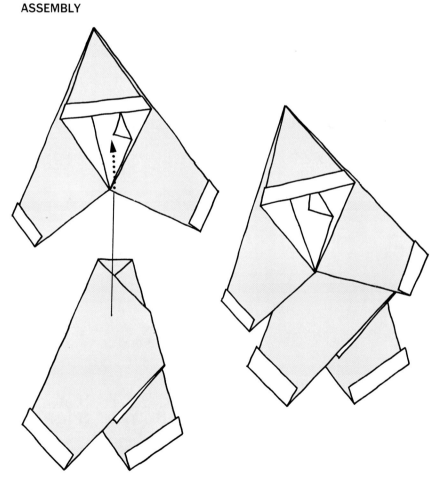

**1** Tuck the Legs between the layers of paper behind the chin.

**2** The Santa Claus complete.

# MOUSE

Animals are often difficult to create using simple folds because most have legs which have to be engineered out of the paper square. However, a mouse is a compact shape and easier to fold. Not surprisingly, it is a popular subject among origami creators. For my design here, use a square of thin paper which has the same colour on both sides. A 15 cm (6 in) square of paper will make a life-sized mouse.

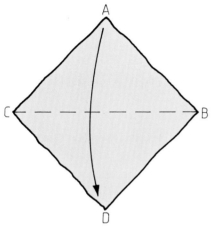

**1** Fold A down to D.

**2** Fold C across to B. Unfold.

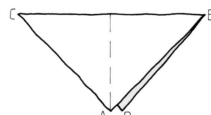

**3** Fold C & B down to AD. (The next drawing is bigger.)

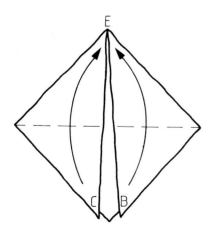

**4** Fold C & B up to corner E.

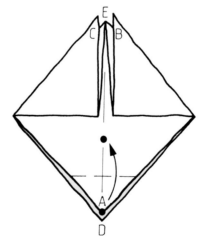

**5** Fold single layer A to the position shown.

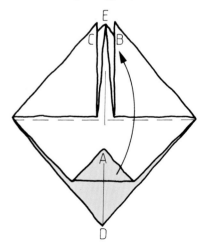

**6** Fold A up on top of CB.

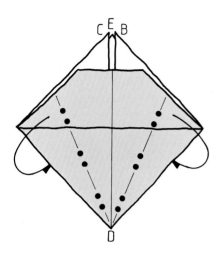

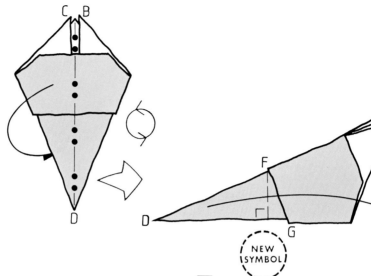

**7** Mountain fold the lower edges behind to make a sharp corner at D. The easy way – you may remember – is to turn the paper over and make a valley fold, then turn over again to the front.

**8** Mountain fold in half. Rotate the paper. (The next drawing is bigger.)

**9** Fold D across to the right, so that the crease drops vertically from point F, forming a right angle with edge DG.

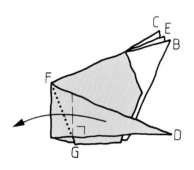

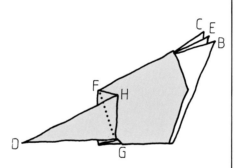

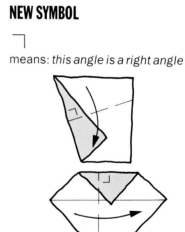

**NEW SYMBOL**

⌐

means: *this angle is a right angle*

**10** Fold D back to the left, with a crease rising vertically from point G.

**11** Tuck point H under the edge that connects F with G . . .

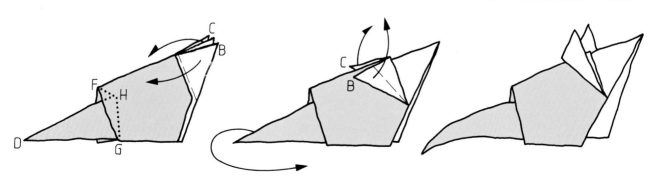

**12** . . . like this. Fold back B & C.

**13** Fold B & C upwards. Curl the mouse tail.

**14** The Mouse complete.

# BRACELET

The origins of this design are obscure, but it is known that the same lock (but made from a longer strip) was used by poor children in the East End of London early this century to make large floor mats out of old sweet wrappers. This version locks only in a line and will not expand widthways to form a mat. Use small 8 x 1 oblongs of thin paper or foil, about 10 x 1.25 cm (4 x ½ in). Begin with a number of 8 x 1 oblongs of two colours, as described above.

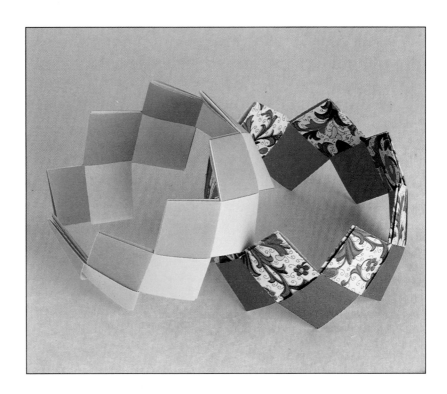

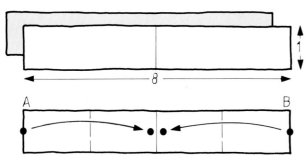

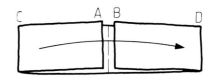

**1** Establish a centre crease. Unfold it. Fold A & B to points a little way from the centre crease. Do not fold them *exactly* to the centre.

**2** Fold C across to D.

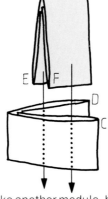

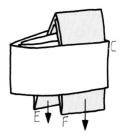

**3** This is the completed module. Simple!

**4** Make another module, but in the second colour. Fold edge F in between the layers at C, and E in between the layers at D . . .

**5** . . . like this. Pull down E & F as far as they will go.

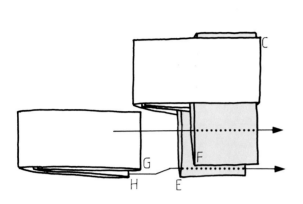

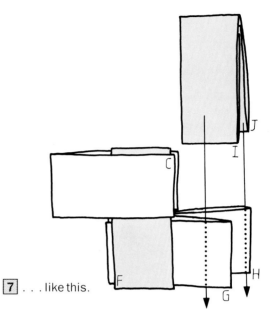

**6** With a module of the first colour, push G through the layers at F, and H through the layers at E . . .

**7** . . . like this.

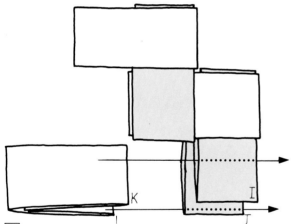

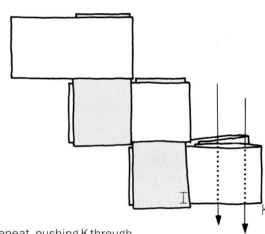

**8** With a module of the second colour, push I through the layers at G, and J through the layers at H.

**9** Repeat, pushing K through I and L through J. Repeat the pattern as often as necessary to make the band the correct length.

**10** To lock the band into a ring, fold a module to Step 3, then unfold the creases at C & D, leaving the centre crease folded. Push this long module through an ordinary module, as described in Step 4, tucking the ends of the long module right into another ordinary module. This will lock the band. Tucking the loose ends right in can be difficult, so you may find it easier to trim the ends of the module, leaving less paper to tuck in. If the lock is weak, glue them in.

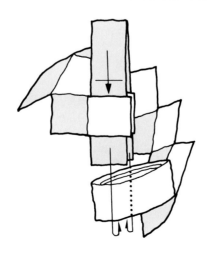

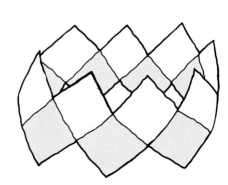

**11** The Bracelet complete.

## WEAVE PATTERNS

Many people would like to create their own designs but think it would be too difficult. This may be true for some, but for many it is possible to adapt an existing technique to create new designs. This is easier than creating a brand new technique and often leads to it. Here then is a traditional technique for creating woven patterns which is infinitely adaptable. Learn the basic technique first, then progress to the patterns suggested later, before experimenting with your own ideas or those in the Creative Suggestions box. Use a strip of duo paper (with different colours or patterns on the two sides) about 2cm (¾ in) wide. Glue pieces together to make a strip as long as is needed.

### BASIC WEAVE BOOKMARK

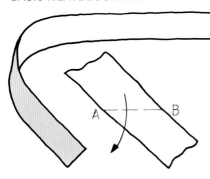

**1** Midway along the length of the strip, fold AB at 45° to the strip so that . . .

**2** . . . the two parts of the strip are at right angles (90°) to each other. Do this by eye, or fold the strip around the outside of a square corner on a piece of paper. Valley fold the coloured part of the strip across to the right, along AC.

**3** Mountain fold along CD, bringing the white part of the strip *on top* of corner C . . .

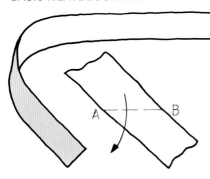

**4** . . . like this. Valley fold the coloured part of the strip to the right along CE.

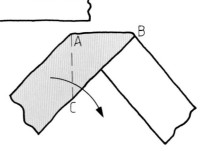

**5** Mountain fold from D, placing the white part of the strip *on top* of E.

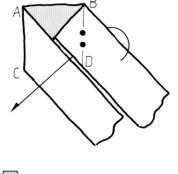

**6** Repeat as often as you wish, valley folding first the coloured part to the right, then mountain folding the white part on top.

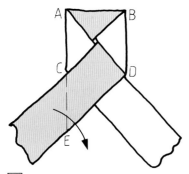

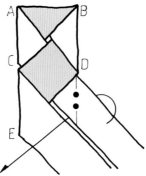

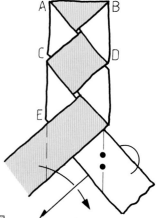

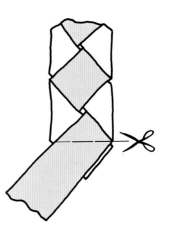

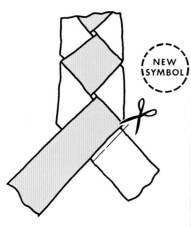

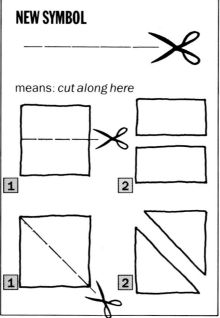

## NEW SYMBOL

— — — — — — — ✂

means: *cut along here*

**1**   **2**

**1**   **2**

**7** To lock the weave, first trim off the white part of the strip as shown . . .

**8** . . . then trim off the coloured part of the strip as shown.

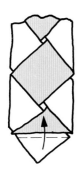

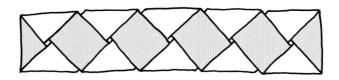

**9** Fold up the white triangle, glueing it to the coloured triangle.

**10** The Bookmark complete.

**TIP**

*Keep checking that all angles are 90°*

## 3-D DECORATION

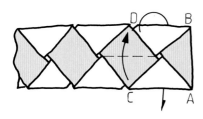

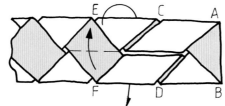

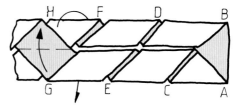

**1** Make a Bookmark as described above. For a longer decoration weave a longer strip. Valley fold C up to D and mountain fold D down to C. A & B also switch position – in effect, the end square swivels back-to-front. Look at Step 2.

**2** Similarly, swivel the second square back-to-front, folding F up to E and E down to F. CA and DB switch position. Look at Step 3.

**3** Repeat with G & H. Note that a continuous slit is growing along the length of the strip.

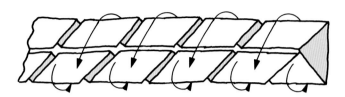

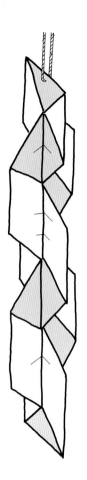

**4** Repeat the swivel technique along the length of the strip. Then twist each swivel to lie at 90° to its neighbours on either side . . .

**5** . . . to look like this seen from the end.

**6** The 3-D decoration complete. Hang it from a thread with lots of others.

## TURNING A CORNER

Weaving a straight strip is fun but limited, so here is an idea for making the strip turn a corner. Once you have mastered it, you will be able to invent many elaborate zig-zag shapes.

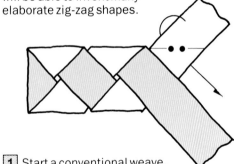

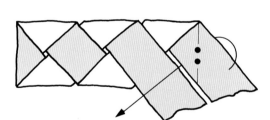

**1** Start a conventional weave. Mountain fold as shown.

**2** Mountain fold the same part of the strip again, placing it on top of the one beneath.

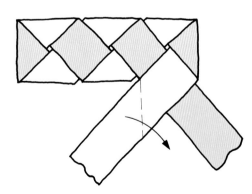

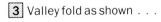

**3** Valley fold as shown . . .

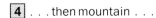

**4** . . . then mountain . . .

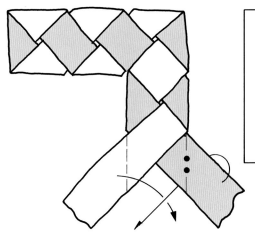

**CREATIVE SUGGESTIONS**

○ Weave a square frame.
○ Weave a mat which has one corner elongating into a strip.
○ Weave a decorative snake.
○ Weave fabric or leather and make a belt to wear.

○ Improvise a fabulously elaborate weave, combining straight strips, corners and mats, all from one strip.
○ Try to find a way of weaving 3-D patterns, not just flat ones.
○ Weave a cube.

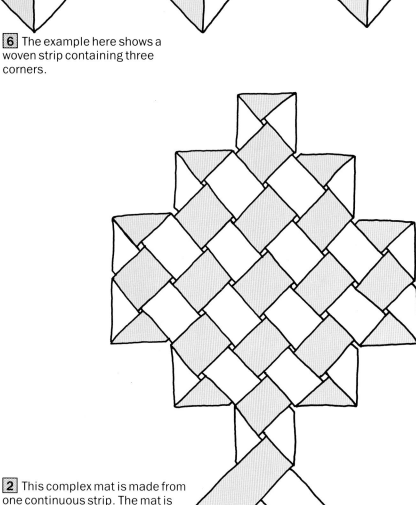

**5** . . . and repeat the conventional valley/mountain folding pattern to weave a straight strip. To turn another corner, repeat Steps 1–4. A woven strip can contain any number of corners, regularly or irregularly spaced.

**6** The example here shows a woven strip containing three corners.

## WOVEN MATS

Strips, straight or zig-zag, are linear weaves – that is, the weave expands in just one direction, forwards. Woven mats weave in two directions, forwards and sideways. Here are two woven mats. They are easier to make than you might think. The key is to fold them neatly.

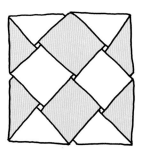

**1** This mat is made using two *separately* woven strips, not one. Can you see the pattern?

**2** This complex mat is made from one continuous strip. The mat is five squares wide; odd-number widths are easier to weave than even-number widths.

# GOLDFISH

There is something undeniably satisfying about making an origami design which inflates when blown into, but sadly there are very few of them. The best-known is the waterbomb, which children are apt to inflate, fill with water and drop from a window! The Goldfish has no such aggressive purpose, though it does follow the same sequence as the waterbomb up to Step 11. Use a 15–20 cm (6–8 in) square of thin or medium-weight paper.

THE DESIGN IS TRADITIONAL

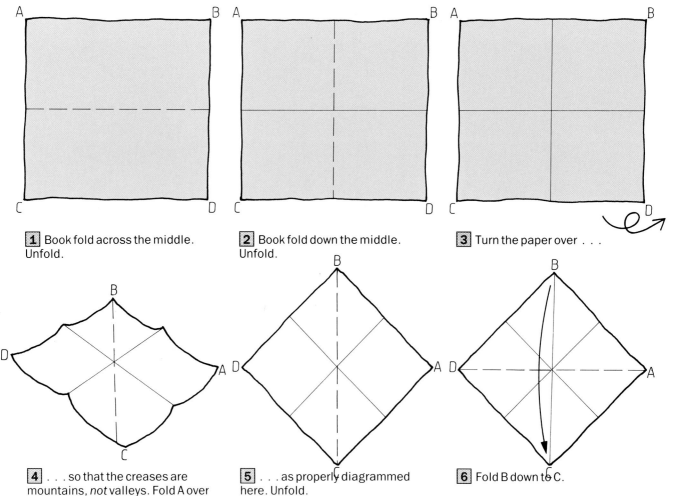

**1** Book fold across the middle. Unfold.

**2** Book fold down the middle. Unfold.

**3** Turn the paper over . . .

**4** . . . so that the creases are mountains, *not* valleys. Fold A over to D, to make a valley diagonal crossing the two mountain book folds . . .

**5** . . . as properly diagrammed here. Unfold.

**6** Fold B down to C.

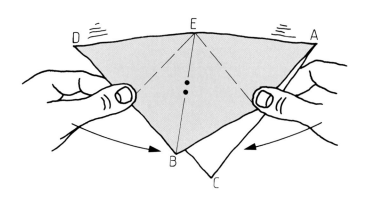

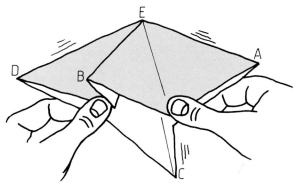

**7** Hold as shown. Swing your hands together, so that . . .

**8** . . . corner B rises towards you and C moves away . . .

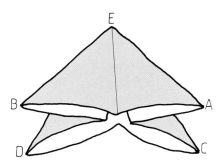

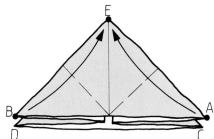

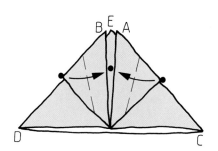

**9** . . . like this. The paper has collapsed to form four double-layer triangles. Flatten B & D to the left and A & C to the right.

**10** In origami, this shape is known as the waterbomb base, from which many different designs can be made. Fold B & A up to E.

**11** Fold dot to dot as shown. Note that the middle dot is a little above the centre.

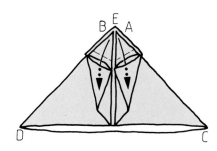

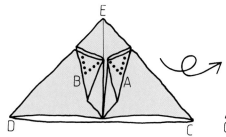

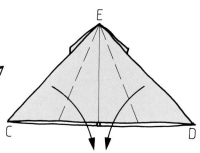

**12** Tuck corners B & A right into the pockets formed between the layers of each triangle . . .

**13** . . . like this. Turn the paper over.

**14** Fold in CE & ED to meet down the centre crease.

ORIGAMI

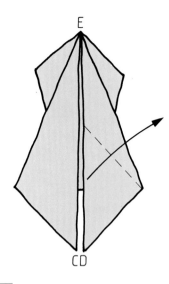

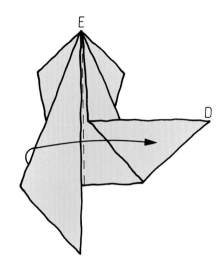

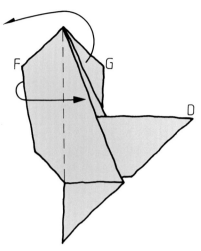

**15** Fold out D.

**16** Swivel C across to the right.

**17** Swivel F to the front and G behind . . .

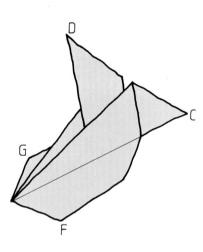

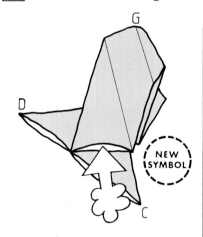

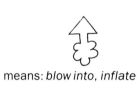

## NEW SYMBOL

means: *blow into, inflate*

**18** . . . to make a 3-D fish shape.

**19** To inflate the goldfish, blow between the layers above C. To do this, put C into your mouth and exhale, so that all your breath goes into the fish. Try not to wet the tail! If the fish does not inflate first time, check that the opening into the fish really is open.

**1**

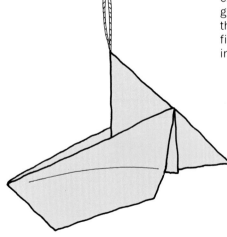

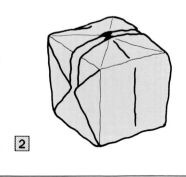

**2**

**20** The Goldfish complete. For display, hang it from a thread attached to the top of the tail.

# SQUASH FOLD DESIGNS

The squash fold technique is one step more advanced than a basic mountain or valley fold. Other advanced techniques will follow in subsequent chapters. It is more complex because, while mountain or valley folds are single creases, a squash fold is more than one crease and requires preparation.

It is not a difficult technique. To help you understand how to make it and also how to recognize and reproduce a squash fold when you see one in the diagrams, it's important to begin with a detailed explanation of the technique. Make the squash fold shown in the Basic example, then do the Exercises before folding the designs which follow.

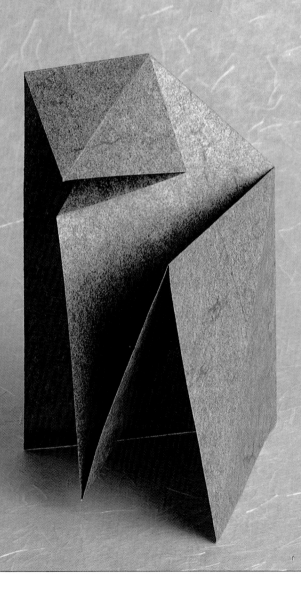

ORIGAMI

# BASIC EXAMPLE OF THE SQUASH FOLD

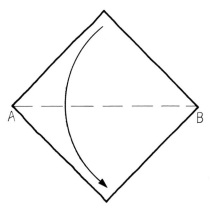

**1** Crease A to B.

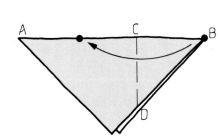

**2** Fold B back along the crease towards A. Its exact placement is unimportant.

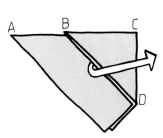

**3** Fold so that crease BC stands upright . . .

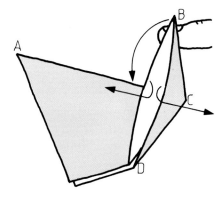

**4** . . . like this. Put pressure on crease BC, separating the layers between B & D and opening the pocket . . . like this. Continue to push so that B drops to touch D.

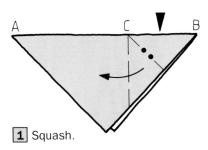

**5** Flatten B against D, and crease CE & CF.

**6** The squash fold complete. It is called a 'squash' because a pocket is opened and squashed flat.

## SUMMARY

The squash fold sequence above has taken six steps to explain. This is unacceptably long so it is condensed into 'before' and 'after' diagrams, see right.

Note that Step 1 of the condensed system shows a valley crease, a mountain crease and the pressure arrow. These three elements are common to all squash fold notations. To make the squash fold from such notation, follow the symbols in this order. First make the valley fold, then partly unfold it, leaving B standing up as in Step 4 of the Basic example. Second, put pressure on crease BC. Lastly squash the pocket flat, making the mountain fold.

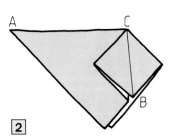

**1** Squash.

**2**

## NEW SYMBOL

▼

means: *apply pressure to this folded edge*

# EXERCISES

Here are a number of squash fold
Exercises included to illustrate the
versatility of the technique and to
help you relate the 'before'
diagram to the 'after'. Work
through them slowly, observing
the rules of folding so far
explained in the book and
following the 'valley-pressure-
squash' sequence explained
previously.

**EXERCISE ONE**

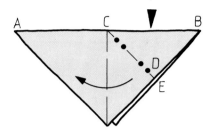 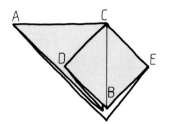

**1** Squash.  **2**

---

**EXERCISE TWO**

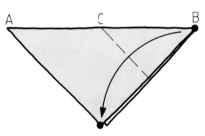 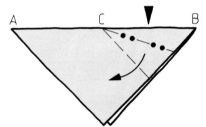 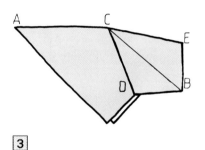

**1** Locate the valley crease.  **2** Squash.  **3**

---

**EXERCISE THREE**

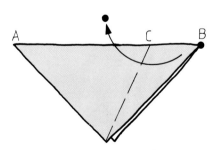 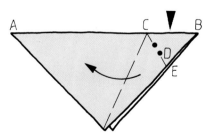 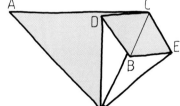

**1** Locate the valley crease.  **2** Squash.  **3**

ORIGAMI

## EXERCISE FOUR

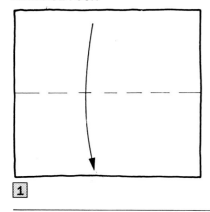

**1**

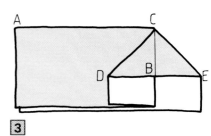

**2** Squash.

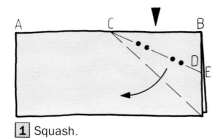

**3**

## EXERCISE FIVE

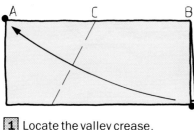

**1** Squash.

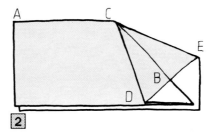

**2**

## EXERCISE SIX

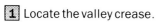

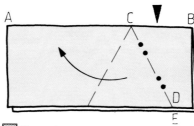

**1** Locate the valley crease.

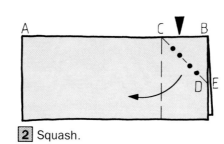

**2** Squash.

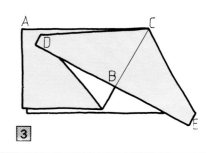

**3**

## EXERCISE SEVEN

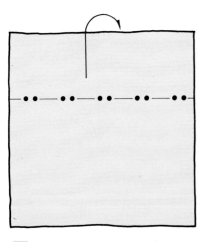

**1**

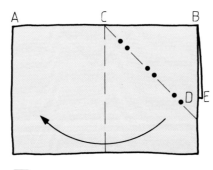

**2** Squash.

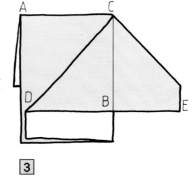

**3**

# PUPPY

This is a simple squash fold design of my own, much liked by young children. The mountain/valley folds should be easy to make if you have worked your way through the preceding chapter, but refer closely to the Basic example of the squash fold when folding the ears. Use two identical squares of paper, not too large. The Puppy made with the first Body will stand upright.

**HEAD**

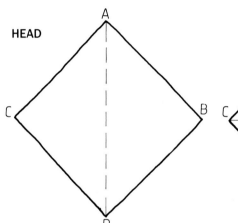

**1** Crease diagonal AD and unfold.

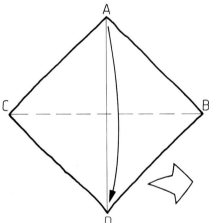

**2** Fold A down to D. (The next drawing is bigger).

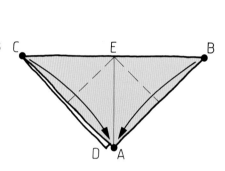

**3** Fold corners C and B down to DA.

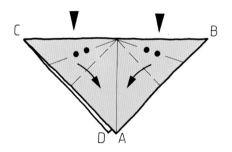

**4** Squash fold as shown.

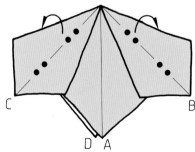

**5** Mountain fold behind the top half of each squash fold.

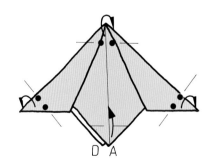

**6** Fold the top of the Head behind. Blunt the tips of the ears. Fold up corner A a little way.

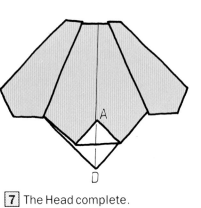

**7** The Head complete.

**BODY ONE**

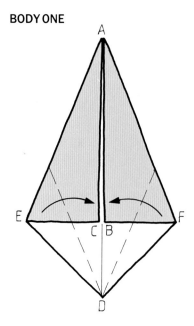

**1** Begin with Step 3 of the Swan (see page 33). Fold in edges ED & FD to lie along the centre crease.

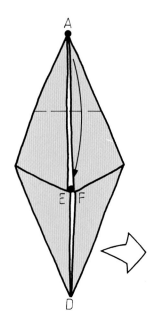

**2** Fold A down to EF. (The next drawing is bigger.)

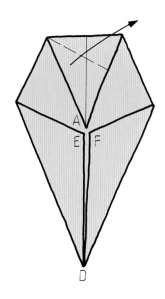

**3** Fold A out to the right . . .

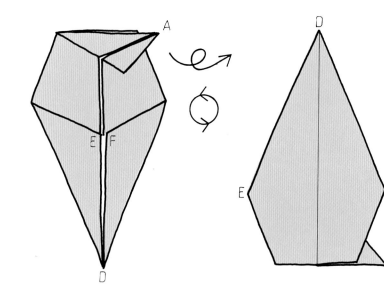

**4** . . . like this. Turn the paper over and rotate.

**5** Body One complete.

**BODY TWO**

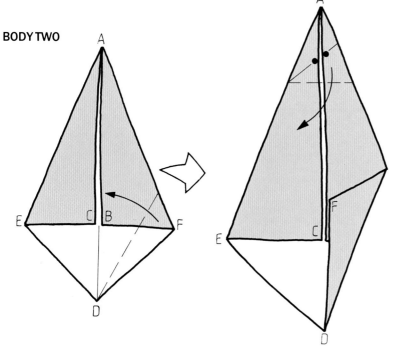

**ASSEMBLY**

**1** Begin as Body One, but fold only edge FD to the centre crease. (The next drawing is bigger.)

**2** Repeat Steps 2—4 of Body One . . .

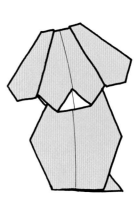

**1** Tuck Body One up in between the layers of the Head . . .

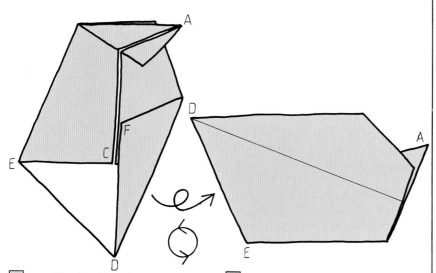

**3** . . . like this. Turn the paper over and rotate.

**4** Body Two complete.

**2** . . . to complete a Standing puppy.

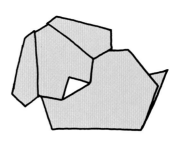

**3** Tuck Body Two up in between the layers of the Head . . . to complete a Sleeping puppy.

ORIGAMI

# CROWN

An origami hat is often an adapted box turned upside down. This hat looks like an upturned Japanese box (see pages 48–50), without the triangular feet turned outwards – but the folding method is totally different! In origami, there are often many ways to fold identical shapes, which means that the beauty of a design can be in the ingenuity of its sequence, not the attractivenesss of the final model. Compare the two sequences and decide which you prefer. Use a double page from a broadsheet (large format) newspaper cut square, or another thin to medium-weight sheet 37–45 cm (15–20 in) square, depending on the size of head it is to fit. I made this design as a variation on a traditional American GI paper-folded hat.

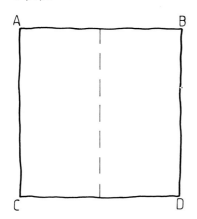

**1** Book fold down the centre. Unfold.

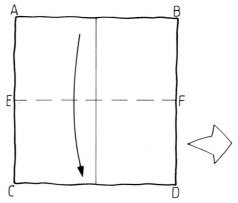

**2** Fold edge AB down to edge CD. (The next drawing is bigger.)

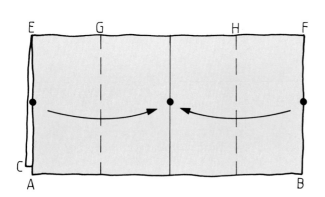

**3** Fold edges EA & FB to the centre crease. Unfold

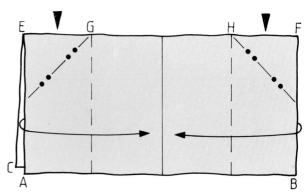

**4** Squash fold, bringing A & B to the centre crease.

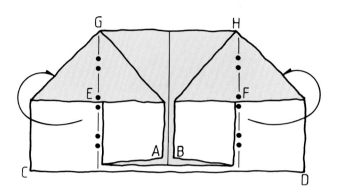

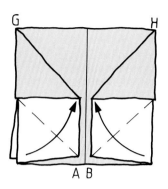

**5** Fold C & D behind.

**6** Fold in the bottom corners .

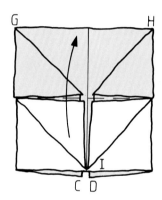

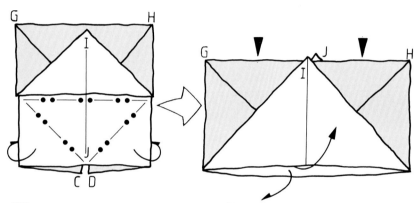

**7** . . . then fold up the new corner I.

**8** Repeat Steps 6 & 7 on the back, to make the paper shape symmetrical front and back. (The next drawing is bigger.)

**9** Open the pocket along the bottom edge and push down on crease GH.

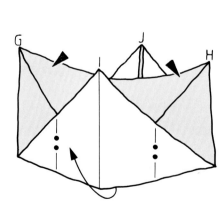

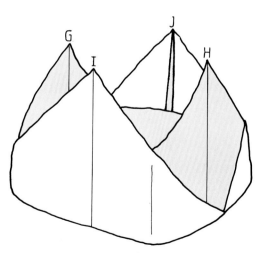

**10** Continue to open the pocket and to flatten the crease against G & H until the crown shape emerges . . .

**11** . . . like this. The Crown complete. Crease down the four sides of the Crown to make it more like a square.

# FLOWER

Most three-dimensional origami flowers (such as the one on pages 118–20) are complex because of the need to engineer a number of sharp, free points from the paper. This flower which I have designed is perhaps the simplest that could be made — a bold claim! The squash folds that it uses are only half creased, which allows the petals to fall outwards in curved, uncreased shapes. Hold the paper exactly as shown in Steps 7–8 and practise forming the petals. Use a small square of paper. The flower will hold a better shape if the paper is dampened before folding so that it dries stiff. Good papers to use for this are those designed to hold water without cockling (wrinkling) such as Ingres paper (Strathmore) or watercolour paper.

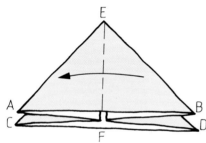

**1** Begin with Step 10 of the Goldfish (see page 69). This shape is the waterbomb base. Fold B & D across to the left.

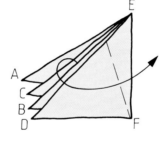

**2** With a crease starting at F, fold B & D back across to the right . . .

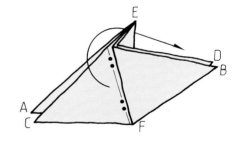

**3** . . . like this. Similarly, mountain fold A & C behind.

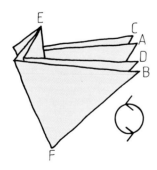

**4** Rotate the paper to the Step 5 position.

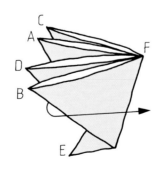

**5** Pull B away from D, A & C.

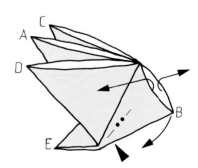

**6** Squash fold B, but only crease *half way* towards BF. To do this . . .

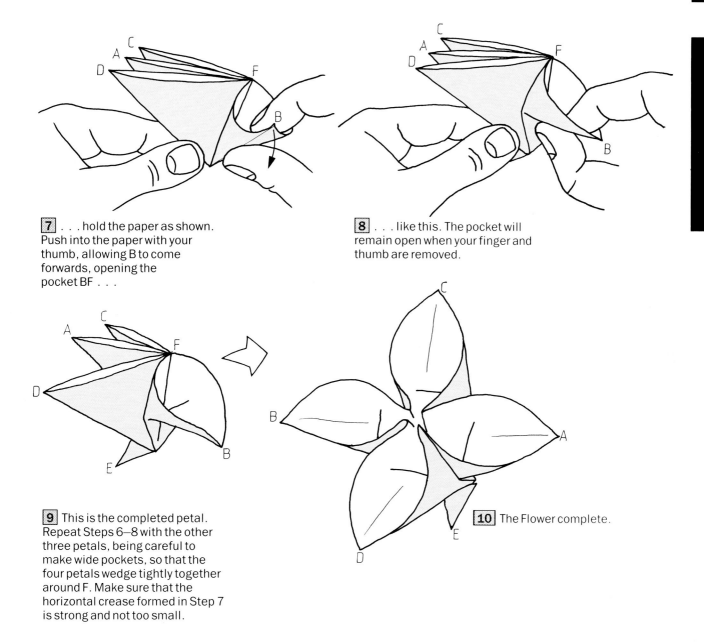

**7** . . . hold the paper as shown. Push into the paper with your thumb, allowing B to come forwards, opening the pocket BF . . .

**8** . . . like this. The pocket will remain open when your finger and thumb are removed.

**9** This is the completed petal. Repeat Steps 6–8 with the other three petals, being careful to make wide pockets, so that the four petals wedge tightly together around F. Make sure that the horizontal crease formed in Step 7 is strong and not too small.

**10** The Flower complete.

---

### CREATIVE SUGGESTION

*Make eight of these flowers and wire them together for a bouquet, using florists' wire and some gutta tape (available from most florists).*

*Cut the florists' wire with pliers, one cut length for each flower, so that each cut length is about twice the height of a bloom. Bend one end of each wire right over to make a hook. Push the straight end down into the bloom and out through point E (Step 10), so that the hooked end catches the paper deep inside.*

*Wrap gutta tape around the wire starting at the straight end, going up to the point where the wire meets the bloom, making a neat turning on the tip of the paper and winding back down the stem. Repeat with all the other blooms except one.*

*Hook the one remaining bloom to a full-length wire and tape up as already described.*

*To attach the short-stemmed blooms to the long main stem, twist a short wire around the long wire near the bloom, binding the two tightly together until both blooms are only a short distance away from the twisted stem, but still on their own separate stems. Repeat, twisting short wires on to the long one and alternating them so that if one bloom comes off on the left, the other comes off on the right, then left, then right and so on.*

*Place the main stem inside a vase and bend the wires so that every bloom can be seen at its best.*

# FALSE NOSE AND MOUSTACHE

This is a marvellous example of impromptu origami nonsense. Made quickly, it is a useful ice breaker at awkward business meetings, parties, lectures and so on and is guaranteed to raise a giggle. Try to memorize it. Wear one next time you open your front door to a friend, or hand out a few at a boring meeting! Use a 10 cm (4 in) square of duo paper.

DESIGN BY GABRIEL ALVAREZ (SPAIN)

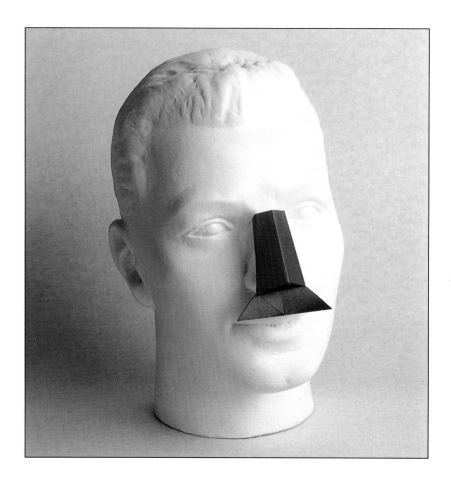

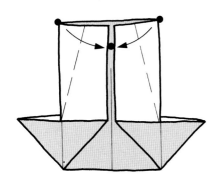

**1** Begin with Step 9 of the Butterfly. Fold A & B to the centre crease . . .

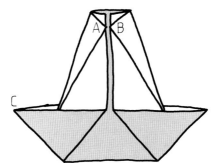

**2** . . . like this. Turn over.

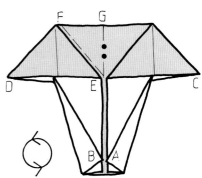

**3** Note E, F & G. Valley fold EF and mountain fold EG. Unfold both.

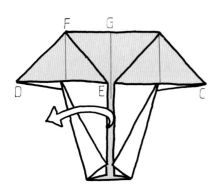

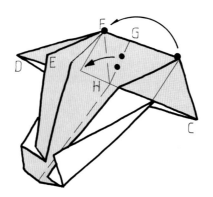

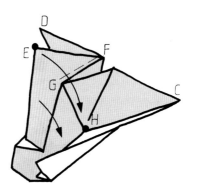

**4** Pull up corner E.

**5** Refold the Step 3 creases, folding dot to dot and making a V-shaped pleat to the left of centre. The paper will become three-dimensional and will not lie flat.

**6** Refold E back on top of the pleat, trapping it in place. Let E touch H.

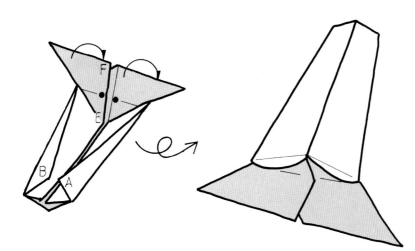

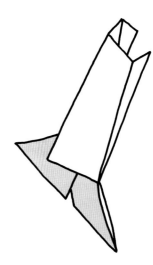

**7** Mountain fold as shown. Turn over.

**8** The False nose and moustache complete.

**9** This is the view from the side, showing the overhang formed by the nose. It also shows flaps A & B which will grip your nose to hold the design firmly in place. If it falls off, tuck the top of the nose under the bridge of a pair of spectacles, where it will stay!

# STRAWBERRY

The shape at Step 8 is the waterbomb base (see pages 68–9) turned inside out, with the crease pattern remaining the same. This new shape is called the preliminary fold, so-called because other bases are developed from it. This Strawberry appears to contain many steps, but from Step 8 onwards everything is simply repeated four times. The design has eight layers at Step 17, so it is important to keep turning over the correct number of layers to find the next face to be folded. Try to keep four layers either side of the centre — this will balance the thicknesses of paper and make folding more accurate. Use a small square of red/green duo paper, or red and green squares folded back to back. It is easier to fold them separately, then slot one into the other at Step 17, than to fold them back to back from the start.

DESIGN BY RAE COOKER (USA)

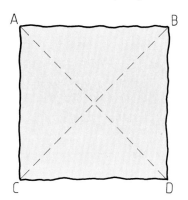

**1** Fold one diagonal. Unfold. Crease the other. Unfold.

**2** Turn the paper over.

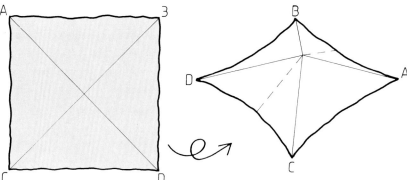

**3** All creases are now mountains. Make a valley book fold through the centre. Unfold.

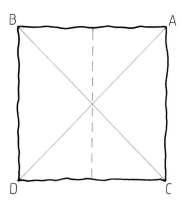

**4** In diagram form, this is how it would be notated.

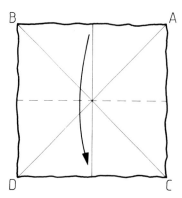

**5** Fold BA down to DC.

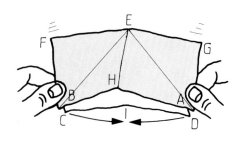

**6** Hold as shown, and swing your hands towards each other . . .

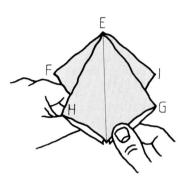

**7** . . . like this. The shape will have four double-layer triangles, all meeting at E. Flatten the paper, so that I & G lie on the right and E & G lie on the left.

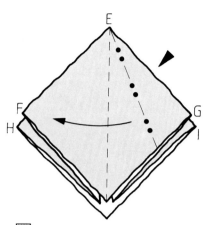

**8** This shape is called the preliminary fold. Squash fold crease EG, here shown in condensed notation. Refer back to the Exercises if you need to refresh your memory.

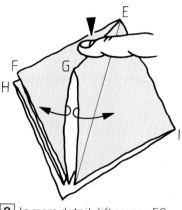

**9** In more detail, lift crease EG. Put your finger on the crease and push . . .

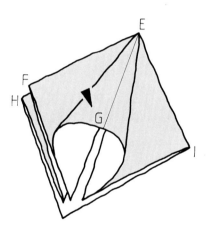

**10** . . . like this. Keep pushing . . .

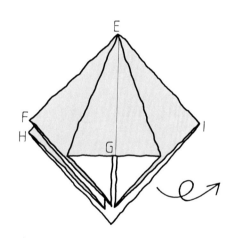

**11** . . . to flatten the squash fold. This shape is the result of the condensed notation shown back in Step 8. Turn the paper over.

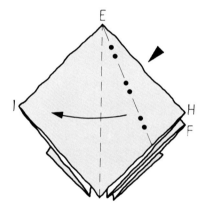

**12** Repeat Steps 8–11 with crease EH . . .

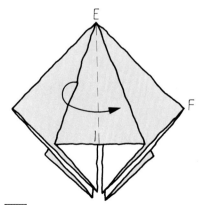

**13** . . . like this. Fold the left half of the squashed triangle over to the right.

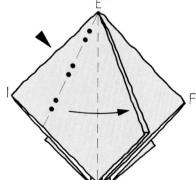

**14** Squash fold crease EI . . .

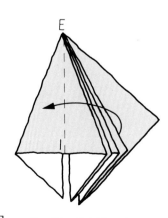

**15** . . . like this. Fold four layers on the right across to the left.

ORIGAMI

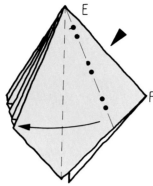

**16** Squash fold crease EF . . .

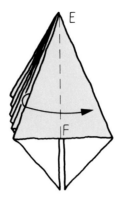

**17** . . . like this. Fold one layer on the left across to the right, to expose . . .

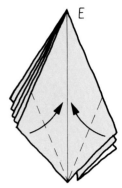

**18** . . . a blank face. Fold in the short edges.

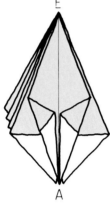

**19** Repeat on the other three blank faces contained within the layers, turning the layers to find them. There are eight layers: try to keep four on either side of the centre.

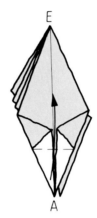

**20** Fold up point A . . .

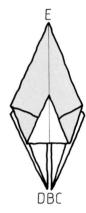

**21** . . . like this. Repeat with D, B & C, turning the layers again as in Step 19.

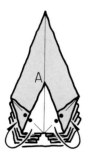

**22** Mountain fold the bottom front layer corners into the blank faces behind.

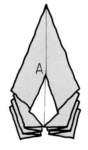

**23** Repeat with the other six corners, turning the layers as described in Step 19. Instead of mountain folding the corners, it may be easier to turn to the blank faces and valley fold them.

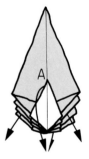

**24** Lift out A, B, C & D. Rotate the paper.

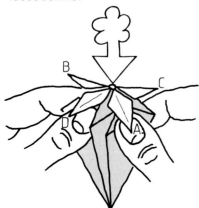

**25** Hold the paper as shown. Blow into the hole to inflate the Strawberry. Allow it to look a little irregular, not too neat.

**26** The Strawberry complete.

# INSIDE AND OUTSIDE
# REVERSE FOLD DESIGNS

The reverse fold is perhaps the most common origami technique after the basic mountain/valley folds and, like mountain/valley folds, the inside and outside variants are identical but opposite.
Like the squash folds described in the previous chapter, reverse folds require preparation. Please make the inside and outside Basic examples described on the next page, then work through the Exercises before folding the designs which follow.

# BASIC EXAMPLE OF THE INSIDE REVERSE FOLD

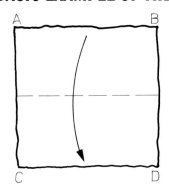

**1** Fold AB down to CD.

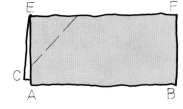

**2** Fold in corner E.

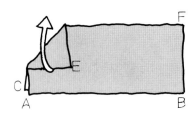

**3** Unfold.

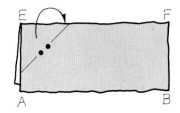

**4** Mountain fold corner E behind, along the Step 2 valley crease.

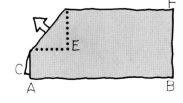

**5** Unfold.

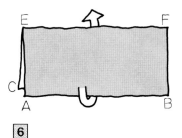

**6**

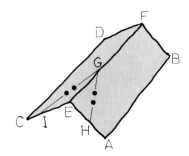

**7** . . . EF is a mountain crease. Make creases IG & GH also mountain creases, forming each in turn.

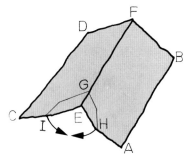

**8** Let crease EG become a valley. Fold the sheet in half along EF, so that H is brought towards I . . .

**9** . . . like this. Let edge AB lie along edge CD. Note corner E between AC.

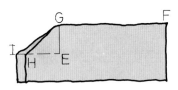

**10** The inside reverse fold complete – so-called because the paper being folded moves *inside* and crease EF is *reversed* from a mountain to a valley between EG.

## SUMMARY

This is how the inside reverse fold is notated: a pressure arrow paired with a mountain fold. Prepare each inside reverse fold by first folding the crease backwards and forwards, as described above in Steps 2–6.

# EXERCISES

**EXERCISE ONE**

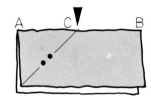

**1** Reverse.    **2**

---

**EXERCISE TWO**

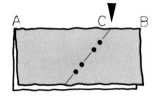
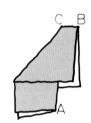

**1** Reverse.    **2**

---

**EXERCISE THREE**

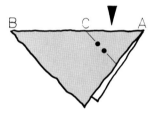
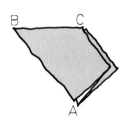

**1** Reverse.    **2**

---

**EXERCISE FOUR**

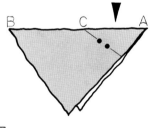
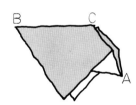

**1** Reverse.    **2**

---

**EXERCISE FIVE**

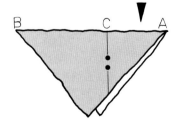
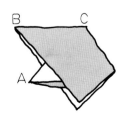

**1** Reverse.    **2**

# BASIC EXAMPLE OF THE OUTSIDE REVERSE FOLD

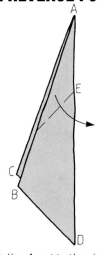

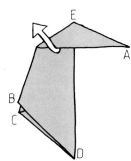

**1** Begin with Step 3 of the Swan (see page 33). Fold B across to C.

**2** Valley A out to the right . . .

**3** . . . like this. Unfold.

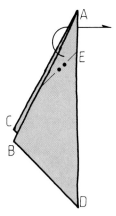

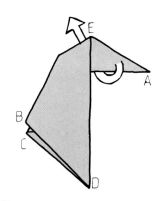

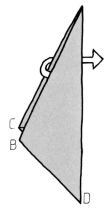

**4** Mountain fold A behind along the Step 2 crease.

**5** Unfold.

**6** Pull C round the back to the right, to give the Step 1 shape seen from the other side.

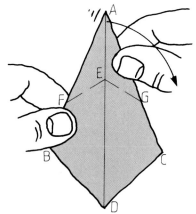

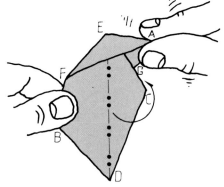

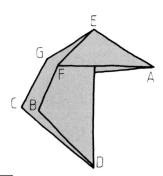

**7** Hold as shown, creasing FE & EG as valley creases, forming each in turn. Pull A forward . . .

**8** . . . creasing CD as a mountain, so that the paper folds in half right down the middle. Keep pulling A forwards along the Step 6 creases.

**9** The outside reverse fold complete – so-called because the paper being folded (in this example, point A) moves *outside* the remainder of the paper and crease AD is *reversed* from a mountain to a valley between AE.

## SUMMARY

This is how an outside reverse fold is notated: a pressure arrow against the central folded edge with arrows swinging to the front and the rear to show the outward directions in which point A is pulled when the reverse fold is made. Prepare each outside reverse fold by first folding backwards and forwards, as described in Steps 2–5.

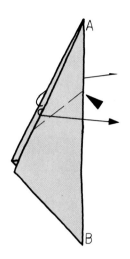

# EXERCISES

**EXERCISE ONE**

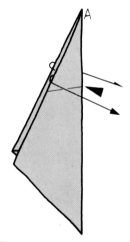

**1** Reverse.

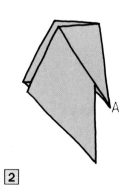

**2**

**EXERCISE TWO**

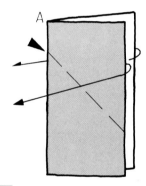

**1** Reverse.

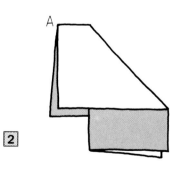

**2**

**EXERCISE THREE**

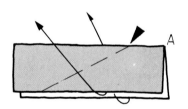

**1** Reverse.

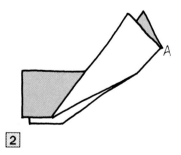

**2**

*ORIGAMI*

### EXERCISE FOUR

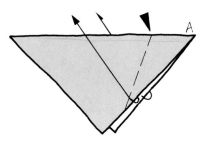

**1** Reverse.

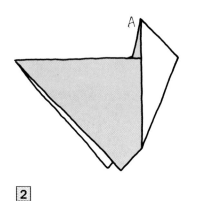

**2**

---

### EXERCISE FIVE

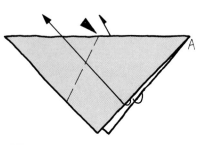

**1** Reverse.

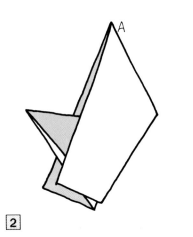

**2**

## IDENTICAL BUT OPPOSITE

In some instances, a reverse fold may equally well be folded as an inside reverse or an outside reverse, because the result is the same, whichever technique is used. Consider this example:

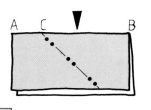

**1** Inside Reverse.

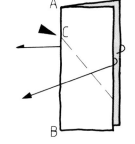

**1** Outside Reverse.

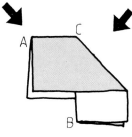

**2**

However, in most instances, one has preference over the other. Consider this example:

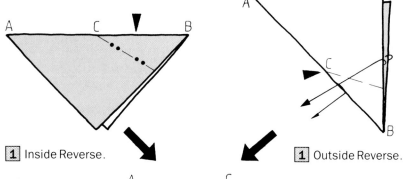

**1** Inside Reverse.

**1** Outside Reverse.

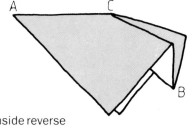

**2**

In this example, the inside reverse is easier to make than the outside reverse, because less paper has to be manipulated. So, although the inside and outside reverse folds are fundamentally identical, one will usually be easier to make than the other. This is the one given in the diagrams.

# FOUR FEEDING BIRDS

These birds are perhaps an extreme example of just how stylized origami can become. With only a few folds the representation of a feeding bird can be made, rather in the way that a cartoonist can draw a likeness of a person with just a few deft strokes of a pen. Some would say that because these birds are so simple they are hardly origami at all, while others would argue that to capture the pose of a bird with a few folds is more elegant than to do so with many folds. Whatever their status, the birds are included here because they use the inside and outside reverse folds to good effect. I designed all the birds except Method Two, which is traditional Japanese. Use small squares, the same colour both sides, or duo paper.

**METHOD ONE**

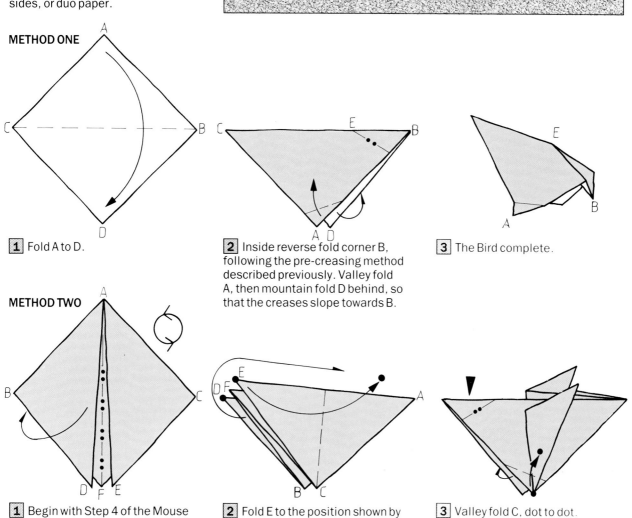

**1** Fold A to D.

**2** Inside reverse fold corner B, following the pre-creasing method described previously. Valley fold A, then mountain fold D behind, so that the creases slope towards B.

**3** The Bird complete.

**METHOD TWO**

**1** Begin with Step 4 of the Mouse (see page 60). Mountain fold B behind. Rotate the paper.

**2** Fold E to the position shown by the dot near A. Repeat behind with D.

**3** Valley fold C, dot to dot. Repeat behind with B. Reverse F.

ORIGAMI

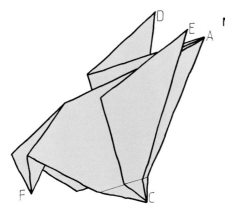

**METHOD THREE**

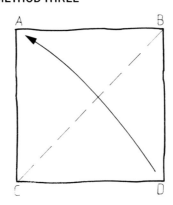

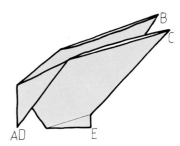

**4** The Bird complete.

**1** Fold D to A.

**2** Fold C to B. (The next drawing is bigger.)

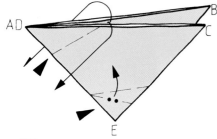

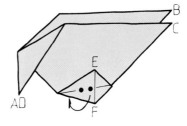

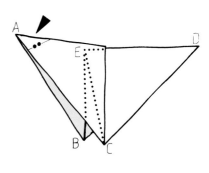

**3** Squash fold E. Outside reverse corner D, following the pre-creasing method described above.

**4** Fold F behind to create a foot either side of the Bird.

**5** The Bird complete.

**METHOD FOUR**

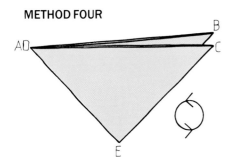

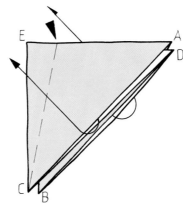

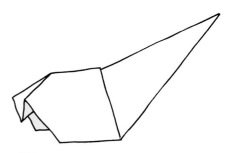

**1** Begin with Step 3 of Method 2. Rotate the paper.

**2** Outside reverse fold corner A to the position shown in Step 3. This may be a little tricky – unfolding the paper will help.

**3** Note the X-ray position of E. Reverse A.

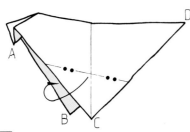

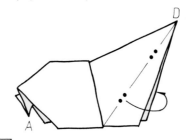

**4** Mountain fold C inside. Repeat behind with B.

**5** Narrow the tail.

**6** The Bird complete.

# SNAIL

Like the Mouse (see pages 60–1), snails are a popular origami subject because of their compact shape. This version is one of the simplest snails yet designed. Some of the more complex versions include two long antennae and three-dimensional shells complete with spiral – all that's missing is the slime! Use small squares of thin paper, or experiment with thicker, textured papers.

DESIGN BY ALFREDO GIUNTA (ITALY)

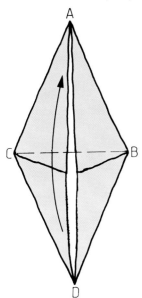

**1** Begin with Step 2 of the Puppy, Body One (see page 76). Fold D to A.

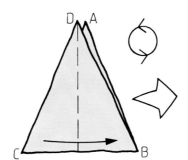

**2** Fold C to B. Rotate the paper. (The next drawing is bigger.)

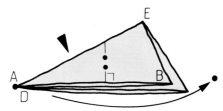

**3** Reverse fold AD to the dot near C. (The next drawing is bigger.)

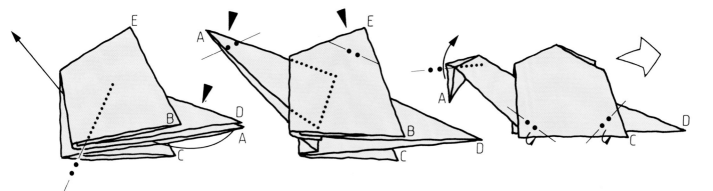

**4** Reverse fold A with a crease made inside the shell. Look at the next step to see the shape you are trying to achieve. Note that D does not move.

**5** Reverse A & E.

**6** Round off the shell at the bottom. Reverse A back up to suggest the antennae and the snail is complete.

# BUTTERFLY RING

The Japanese paperfolder who designed this delightful fold was blinded at an early age. He folds paper because it is an activity he can do independently of others. A masseur by profession, he travels widely, teaching his numerous creations to sighted and blind pupils alike. He is one of origami's great ambassadors and a true inspiration to all paper folders. Make the ring from a strip of thin paper about 1.2 x 10 cm (½ x 4 in).

DESIGN BY SABURO KASE (JAPAN)

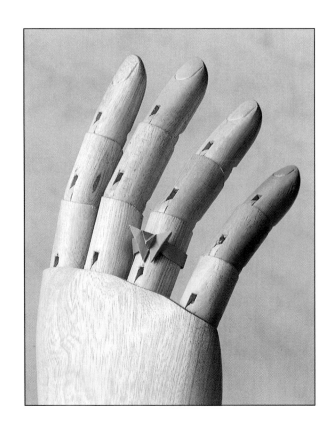

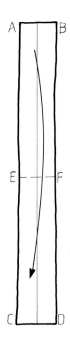

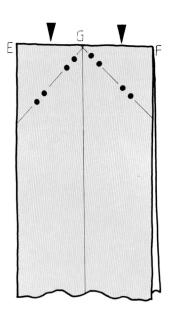

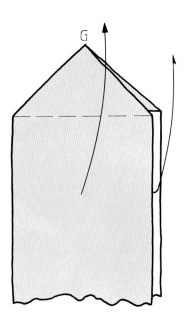

**1** Fold AB to CD, along crease EF. Note that the drawing shows a crease down the centre of the strip which has already been made.

**2** Reverse E & F.

**3** Fold up the front strip along a crease which follows the bottom of the triangle. Repeat behind.

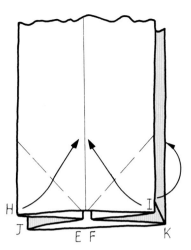

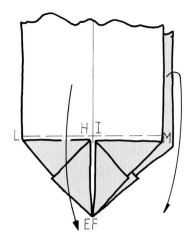

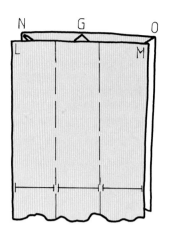

**4** Fold in corners H & I. Repeat behind with J & K.

**5** Fold the strip back down along LM. Repeat behind.

**6** Fold the width of the strip into thirds. Repeat behind.

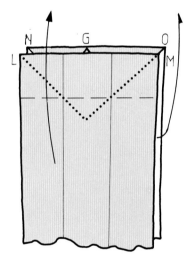

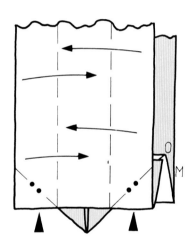

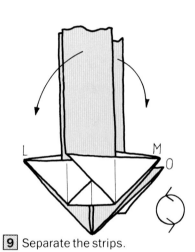

**7** Fold up the strip along a crease made where the third creases made in the previous step cross the triangle hidden inside (shown by the X-ray dots). Repeat behind.

**8** Fold in the sides of the strip, squashing the bottom edges to make triangles. Repeat behind.

**9** Separate the strips.

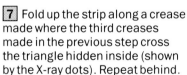

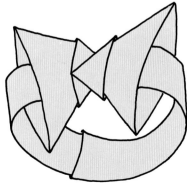

**10** Tuck one end of the strip into the other and adjust to fit.

**11** The Butterfly ring complete.

**CREATIVE SUGGESTION**

*The Butterfly ring is a particularly appropriate gift to give to your partner or sweetheart. Choose an exquisite paper and fold it with great care. You might even memorize the design so that you can fold it while he or she watches.*

# MONKEYS

Double subjects, such as this mother monkey carrying her baby, are rare in origami and are usually very difficult to make. This design, however, is remarkable for its relative simplicity. Some origami creators have argued that to fold double subjects which are not normally joined — such as a one-piece horse and cart — should not be done because it is unnatural. This may be true, but the design presented here is included for its outstanding simplicity and originality. Use a 15–20 cm (6–8 in) square of paper, the same colour both sides.

DESIGN BY DR J. P. WYSEUR (BELGIUM)

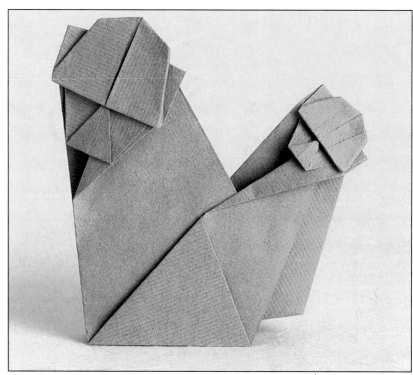

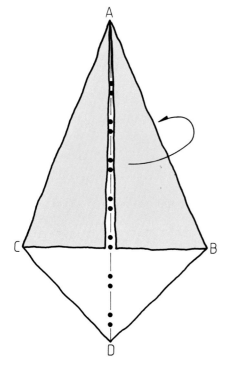

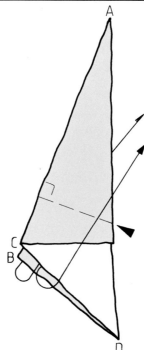

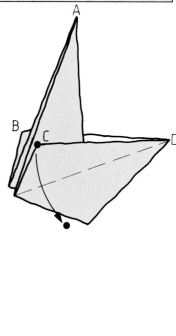

**1** Begin with Step 3 of the Swan (see page 33). Mountain fold B behind.

**2** Outside reverse fold corner D as shown.

**3** Fold down C, dot to dot. Repeat behind with B.

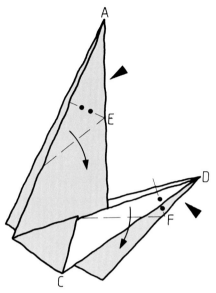

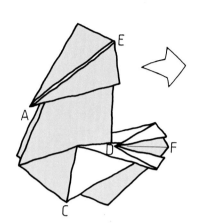

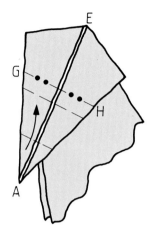

**4** Squash A & D . . .

**5** . . . like this. Refer back to the previous chapter if you need a squash fold refresher. (The next drawing is bigger.)

**6** Fold up tip A and pleat G to H.

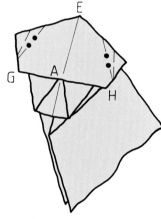

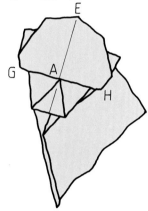

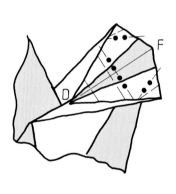

**7** Pleat the ears . . .

**8** . . . to complete the head.

**9** Repeat Steps 6–8 with D

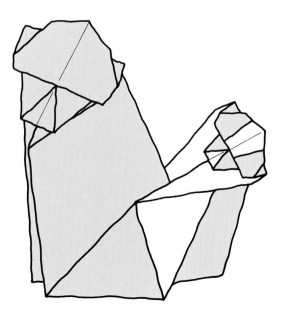

**10** The Monkeys complete.

# REVERSE FOLD ALPHABET

This is one of those designs with a great capacity for variation. Learn the basic principle by folding the letter A, then B, then attempt some of the letters in the rest of the alphabet. Use a strip of thin paper, at least six times as long as it is wide for the simpler letters (e.g. L, V, T), or about 10 times as long as it is wide for more complex letters (e.g. B, E, W). Computer tape is good for large letters, as is till or 'tally' tape — the tape used in cash registers on which your receipt is printed. Smaller letters can be made from 2.5 cm (1 in) wide strips cut from sheets of writing or typing paper, or indeed almost any other type of paper. The designs are my own, but many others have been invented.

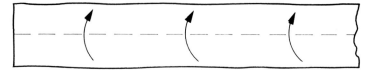

For all letters valley fold the strip in half.

**LETTER A**

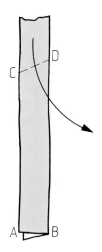

**1** Near end AB, make crease CD, bringing the remainder of the strip across to the right . . .

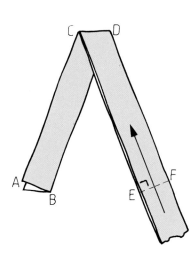

**2** . . . like this. Crease E to F across the strip.

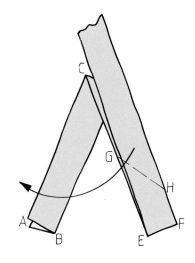

**3** Crease G to H, swinging the remainder of the strip across to the left in the correct position to form the horizontal bar of the A.

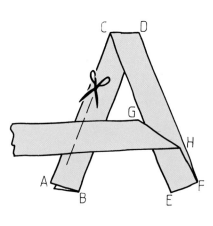

**4** Cut off the excess paper.

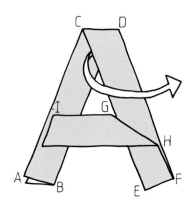

**5** Unfold back to Step 1.

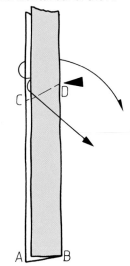

**6** Outside reverse the strip at CD.

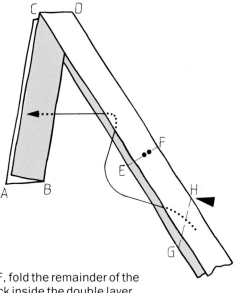

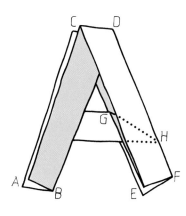

**7** At EF, fold the remainder of the strip back inside the double layer of paper between EF & CD, then reverse along GH to form the horizontal bar. Tuck it behind the left-hand upright.

**8** The letter A complete. Note that up to Step 5 all the creases are valleys or mountains. These creases establish the basic shape of the letter before the reverse folds are made. This is the procedure for every letter.

## LETTER B

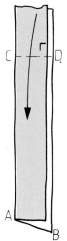

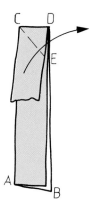

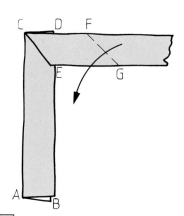

**1** Near end AB, make crease CD to double the paper back over AB.

**2** Fold the strip out 45° along crease CE . . .

**3** . . . then down along crease FG.

**4** Continue to fold the strip backwards and forwards with a series of valley folds as shown, until the shape of the letter is complete. Take care to do it accurately, so that the letterform looks attractive. Note that the top half of the letter is more condensed than the bottom half. Cut off the excess paper when the strip has returned to AB. Unfold back to Step 1.

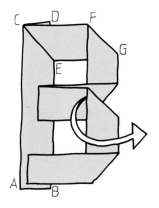

ORIGAMI

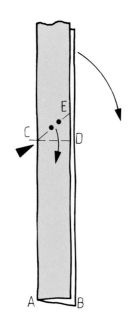

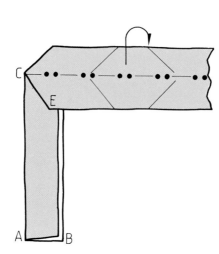

**5** Squash along existing creases, flattening out the centre crease down the strip, then . . .

**6** . . . mountain fold in half again.

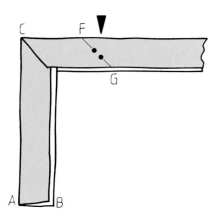

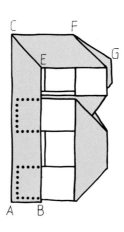

**7** Reverse along FG.

**8** Continue to make inside and outside reverse folds at the existing valley folds. Tuck the horizontal bars in between the layers of the strip between AB & CE. The letter B is complete.

## LETTERS C – Z

All these letters are made in the same way as the A and B letters:

**1** Fold the strip in half.

**2** Valley fold the strip backwards and forwards in the shape of the required letter.

**3** Cut off the excess paper.

**4** Unfold back to a long strip folded down the middle.

**5** Form inside and outside reverse folds at the valley creases, to complete each letter.

*Note:* It is important: that the crease that folds the strip in half is placed either to the left or right of the strip when the valley creases are made. For example, the central crease runs down the left-hand vertical edge of the letter C. If it were on the right, all the outside reverses would be inside reverses, and vice-versa. The silhouette of the letter would be unaffected, but the layering of the paper at the corners would be different, creating a different surface design.

---

### TIP

*To ensure that all the letters are the same height, draw two parallel lines on a sheet of paper which are the same distance apart as the height of the letter you wish to fold. Valley fold the strip against the sheet – not in the air – so that you can measure the height of the letters against the lines and so put each fold in the correct place.*

CDEFG
HIJKLM
NOPQR
STUVW
XYZ

## VARIATIONS

The alphabet shown above is an example of basic folding design. With more sophisticated folding, the letter forms can become more complex. Here are three examples:

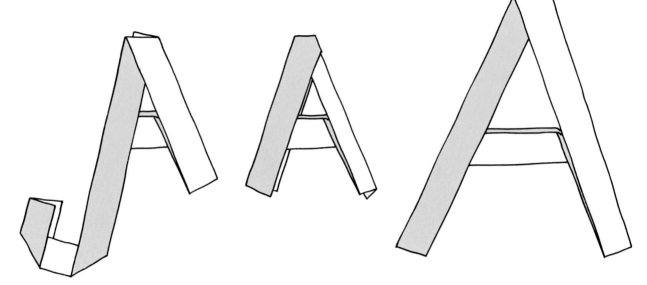

**1** Add curled ends to some of the letters, particularly those at the beginning of a word. These decorative elements can be elaborated to become very ornate, rather like medieval calligraphy.

**2** Fold some of the strokes in half to narrow them, but do so in a consistent way. For example, fold all the right-hand verticals in half (as shown here), or all the left-hand ones, or even all the horizontals.

**3** Use very long strips and make large, thin letters.

### CREATIVE SUGGESTIONS

○ Create numerals and punctuation marks to add to the alphabet. Make sure that everything is in the same style.

○ Create a lower case alphabet without any capital letters. Capital letters are upper case.

○ Using a very long strip of computer tape or till tape, fold all the letters in a word from just one piece! This will be very effective on the front of a birthday card, spelling out someone's name. For a child, fold the age.

○ The strip-folding technique can be applied to any shape which can be drawn without taking the pencil off the paper, even if it means doubling back along a line, like some of the letters do. Thought of in this way, it is possible to fold any shape from a strip, such as a face, a building, a space station, a horse, a radish . . to name but a few. Anything goes! Draw them first using a continuous line, then fold.

○ One continuous strip idea is the word 'Origami', drawn here with a capital O and the remaining letters lower case. See if you can fold it, first by folding large thin letters, then by folding smaller, chunkier ones, which is more difficult.

○ Rather than making reverse folds all the time, just fold the initial mountain/ valley creases. This will not create as stable a structure as a reverse folded strip, but it is much easier.

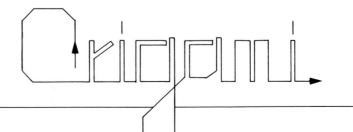

# SIX-POINTED STAR

The natural angles that can be
made by folding a square are 90°,
45°, 22.5° and so on, while the
angles used in the Six-pointed star
are 120° and 60°. The problem is
to find a way to fold these angles
from a square. Fortunately, there
is a simple and elegant way to do
this, which can be seen in Steps
1–4. In fact, there are many
wonderful methods to make
geometric shapes or
constructions by folding, which
would otherwise have to be made
using a protractor, ruler and pair of
compasses. See, for example, the
method for making a Pentagon on
pages 118–20. The geometry of
folding is a profound and beautiful
subject, currently being explored
by many creative paperfolders.
Use a square of thin paper or
paper-backed metallic foil.

DESIGN BY SHUZO FUJIMOTO (JAPAN)

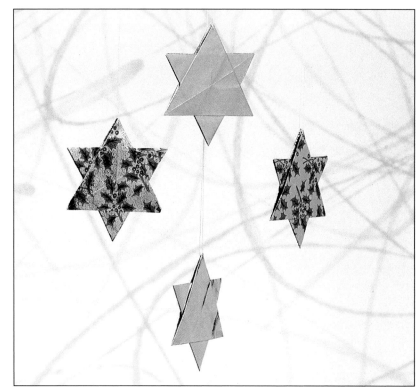

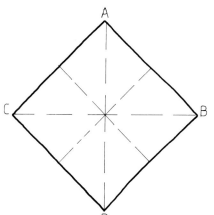

**1** Crease and unfold both
diagonals and book folds.

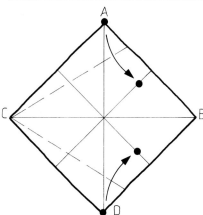

**2** Fold A on to the book fold
crease, so that the crease
originates at C. Repeat with D.
Keep it neat.

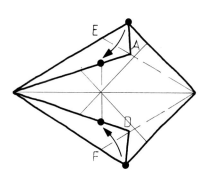

**3** Fold dot to dot, so that crease
EB passes through corner A, and
crease FB passes through D.

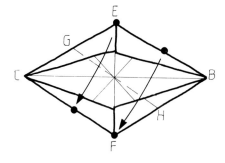

**4** Fold edge EB across to lie on
edge CF . . .

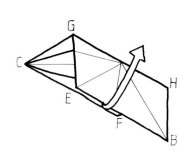

**5** . . . like this. Unfold.

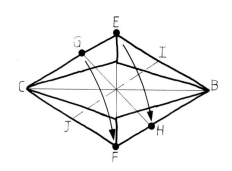

**6** Repeat, folding edge CE
across to EB. Unfold.

ORIGAMI

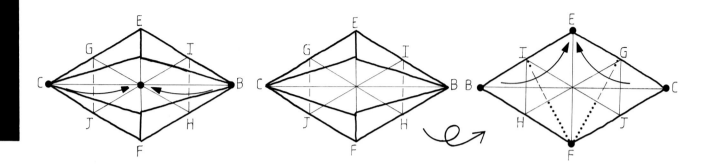

**7** Fold C & B to the middle. Unfold.

**8** This is the crease pattern. Turn over.

**9** Put B on E, but press and crease only where the crease passes across crease BC. If continued, the crease would run from I to F. Repeat, putting C on E, then press and crease across BC. These are location points used in Steps 10 & 11.

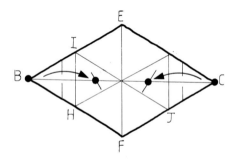

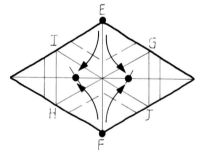

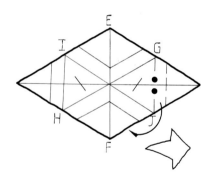

**10** Fold B & C to the location creases just made. Unfold.

**11** Fold corner E to each location crease in turn, but creasing only from the edge to the crease running between E & F. Repeat, folding corner F to each location crease in turn.

**12** Follow existing creases to make a mountain/valley pleat near C.

ORIGAMI

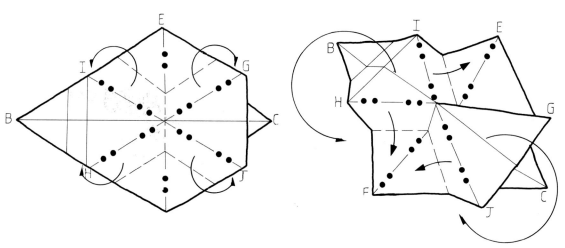

**13** Strengthen the marked creases, looking carefully to see which creases are mountains and which are valleys. The paper will start to collapse . . .

**14** . . . like this. Allow it to collapse so that HI moves to lie behind JG. As the paper collapses, allow the layers to pass by each other beneath K.

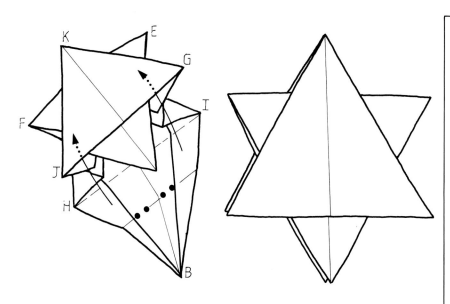

**15** Pleat as in Step 12, tucking the pleat into edge JG. This will lock the star shape and hold it flat.

**16** The Six-pointed star complete. Note that the reverse folds used in this design are made in Steps 13–15, along creases IKG & HKJ. Smaller reverse folds are made nearer E & F, so that the two together form a type of pleated reverse fold, rather like the line of pleated reverse folds seen in the Fallen leaves which follow.

**CREATIVE SUGGESTIONS**

○ Make a large number of stars using metallic foil and suspend them from the ceiling at different heights to create a spectacular 'sky at night'. Invent a man in the moon or space ship to complete the scene.

○ Make a star, attach it to a length of thin thread and write a message on one side. Give it to a friend as a novel Christmas card which can be hung on the tree.

# FALLEN LEAVES

This design of mine features a line of inside reverse folds made all the way from the stalk to the tip of the leaf. Avoid spacing them too regularly and neatly, because this will not accurately represent the irregular shape of a fallen leaf. Use a small square of paper. Experiment with thick sheets lightly dampened before folding. Make soft creases.

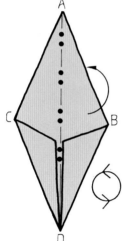

**1** Begin with Step 2 of the Puppy, Body One (see page 76). Mountain fold B behind. Rotate the paper.

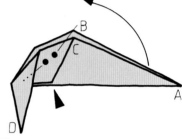

**2** Outside reverse D as shown.

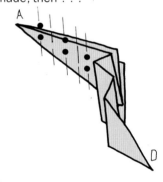

**3** Inside reverse A, close and parallel to the outside reverse just made, then . . .

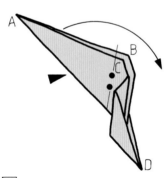

**4** . . . reverse it back . . .

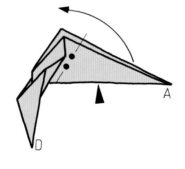

**5** . . . and up again.

**6** Continue to form parallel pleats right up to A, always making just one at a time. Keep the reverse folds close together and go right up to A with them.

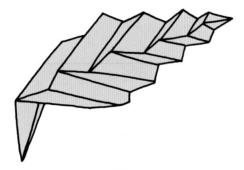

**7** The Fallen leaf complete. Flatten the stalk to one side.

---

### CREATIVE SUGGESTION

*Fold a number of leaves and use them to decorate the table at an autumnal dinner party, buffet or function. The more leaves the merrier.*

# PETAL FOLD DESIGNS

The petal fold is a specialist technique often used, not to create part of the final shape of a design, but to create a basic shape of paper which can then be folded into a number of designs. This is in contrast to, say, the inside reverse fold, which often constitutes part of a final shape, such as the heads on the Feeding birds (see pages 93–4) or the veins on the Fallen leaves (see page 108). The petal fold is most frequently seen when making a shape called a bird base. This is the most versatile of all origami bases, from which thousands of designs have been created. The Flapping birds and Moustache which follow are made from the bird base.
Fold the Basic example — which is the bird base — then work through the Exercises, before folding the designs which follow.

# ORIGAMI

# BASIC EXAMPLE: THE BIRD BASE

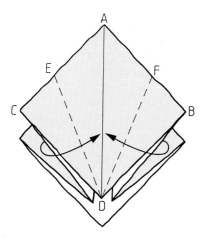

**1** Begin with the preliminary fold, which is Step 8 of the Strawberry (see page 85). The closed corner A is to be at the top. Fold in corners C & B, so that the creases meet at D.

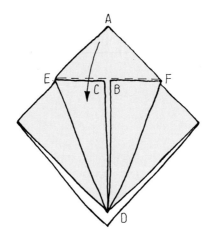

**2** Fold down A over C & B.

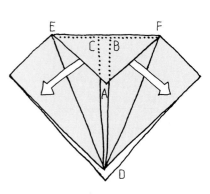

**3** Pull out C & B . . .

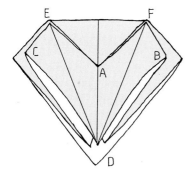

**4** . . . like this.

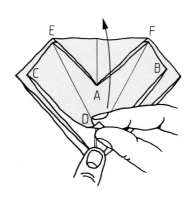

**5** Hold the top layer of corner D between finger and thumb. With your other hand, hold flat the remainder of the layers beneath D and swing D upwards over A . . .

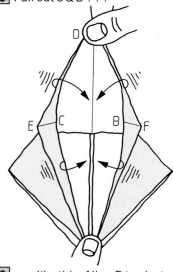

**6** . . . like this. Allow D to pivot along the crease between E & F, as it is pulled further upwards over A. Watch C & B begin to swing inwards . . .

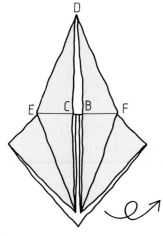

**7** . . . to form a flat diamond shape. Press down on the creases and make a neat point at D. Turn over.

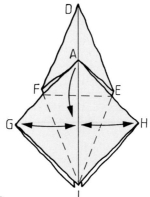

**8** Repeat Steps 1–5 on this side of the preliminary fold. Then . . .

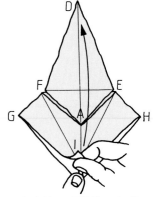

**9** . . . hold I and lift it up to D, repeating Steps 5–7.

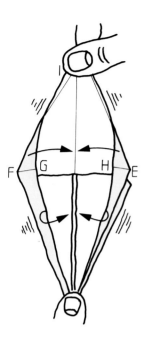

**10** Almost there . . .

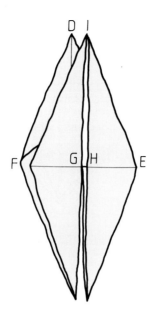

**11** . . . and flatten neatly. The bird base complete. A petal fold has been made on each side of the preliminary fold.

To summarize, a petal fold consists of three preparatory creases: two forming a V-shape, and a third as a horizontal crease across the top of the V. This is how the petal fold made above would be diagrammed:

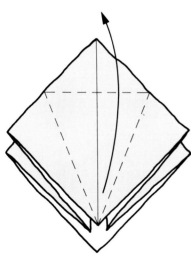

**1** Petal.

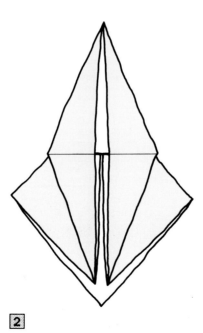

**2**

Learn to recognize the triangle of preparatory creases in anticipation of making a petal fold.

# EXERCISES

All these Exercises begin with the completed squash fold Exercises made on pages 73–4. A petal fold is often preceded by a squash fold, and any squash fold can be petalled. For each Exercise, follow the three-crease pattern shown in the Basic example.

**EXERCISE ONE**

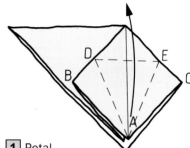

**1** Petal.

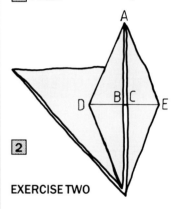

**2**

**EXERCISE TWO**

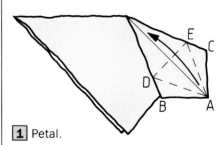

**1** Petal.

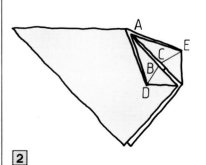

**2**

### EXERCISE THREE

In this Exercise, the top point of the petal is smaller and squatter than the lower part, but A still forms a neat corner. Crease and unfold the long creases first, then crease and unfold the horizontal fold, before lifting corner A and forming the short V-creases to A while petalling.

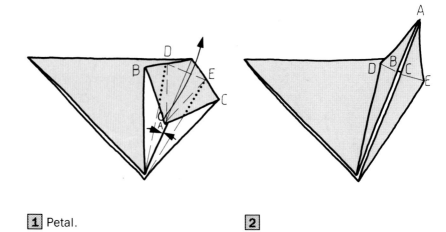

**1** Petal.

**2**

### EXERCISE FOUR

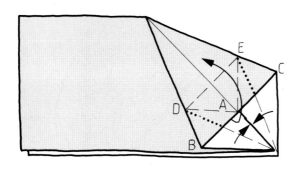

**1** Petal.

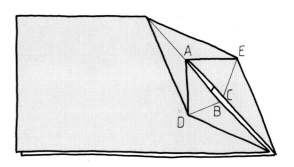

**2**

### EXERCISE FIVE

In this common petal variant, the V-creases have become parallel. Crease and unfold the parallel creases, then crease and unfold the horizontal crease, before lifting A and petalling.

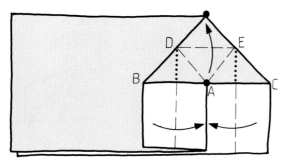

**1** Petal.

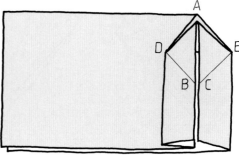

**2**

# TWO FLAPPING BIRDS

Here are two versions of the
traditional Japanese Flapping
bird, thought by many
knowledgeable paperfolders to be
one of the finest designs yet
created. Its structure is
wonderfully direct and simple, and
the wing movements a delightful
surprise. The first version is the
better known. The second is a less
familiar variant, which has a
different and more reliable
mechanism. Use a 15–20 cm
(6–8 in) square of thin paper.

## METHOD ONE

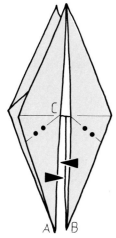

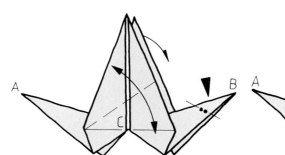

**1** Begin with the bird base.
Inside reverse fold A & B to the
position shown in Step 2. Note
that the folds meet at C.

**2** Inside reverse fold B to form
the head. Valley fold and unfold
the front wing as shown. Repeat
behind.

**3** One Flapping bird complete.

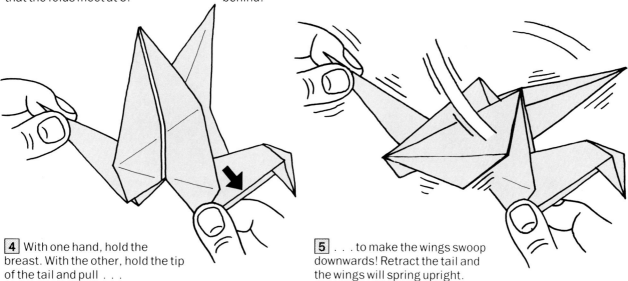

**4** With one hand, hold the
breast. With the other, hold the tip
of the tail and pull . . .

**5** . . . to make the wings swoop
downwards! Retract the tail and
the wings will spring upright.
Repeat.

## METHOD TWO

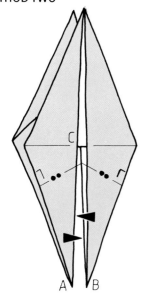

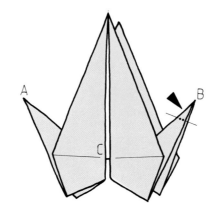

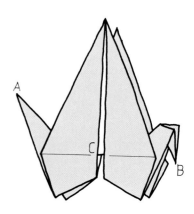

**1** Begin with the bird base. Inside reverse fold A & B, a short distance below C. This distance is important as it influences the flapping mechanism. Don't make it too large or too small.

**2** Inside reverse fold B.

**3** Another Flapping bird complete.

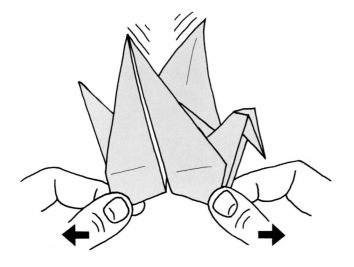

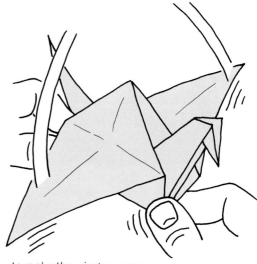

**4** Hold the bottom corners of the bird with both hands as shown, and gently swing them apart . . .

**5** . . . to make the wings swoop downwards! Bring your hands together and the wings will spring upright. Repeat.

---

### CREATIVE SUGGESTION

These birds make ideal impromptu gifts, particularly for children. They are also an ideal way to introduce someone to the delights of origami – the flapping action of the wings is always a great hit. Practise one of the birds until you can fold it automatically, then be prepared to make it at the slightest provocation, or with no provocation at all!

# MOUSTACHE

Compare this delightful fold with the False nose and moustache on pages 82–3. It uses a development of the bird base called, for obvious reasons, the stretched bird base – see Step 6. As with the bird base, the stretched version is also a base from which many designs can be created, particularly simple animals and birds. Use a 10 cm (4 in) square of thin paper and don't forget to blow your nose first!

DESIGN BY JEREMY ADAMSON (ENGLAND)

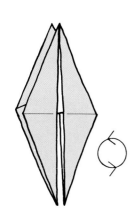

**1** Turn the bird base upside down.

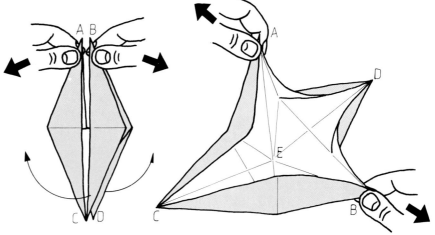

**2** Hold tightly as shown. Swing your hands apart, allowing C & D to rise gracefully . . .

**3** . . . like this. Note E in the centre of the paper. Hold on to the A & B corners very tightly and pull your hands quickly apart. The aim is to make diagonal crease AEB into a continuous mountain fold . . .

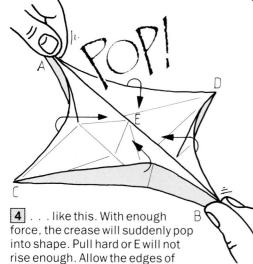

**4** . . . like this. With enough force, the crease will suddenly pop into shape. Pull hard or E will not rise enough. Allow the edges of the paper to collapse towards E, C & D will begin to rise.

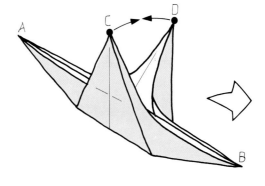

**5** Flatten the paper, making new creases. Let C touch D. (The next drawing is bigger.)

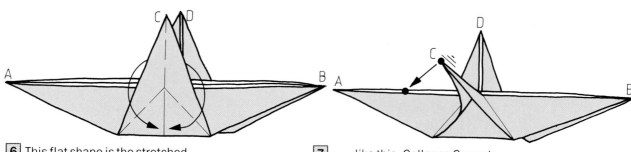

**6** This flat shape is the stretched bird base. Make three creases simultaneously as shown, bringing together the edges meeting at C . . .

**7** . . . like this. Collapse C over to the left, flattening it dot to dot.

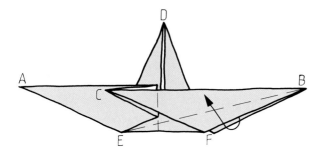

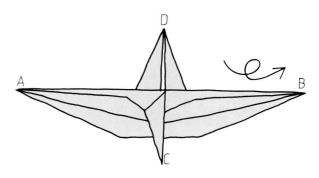

**8** Fold in corner F with a crease that runs between E & B. Keep it neat.

**9** Similarly, fold in corner E, tucking it under the arm near C.

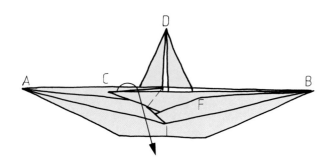

**10** Fold down C . . .

**11** . . . like this. Turn the paper over.

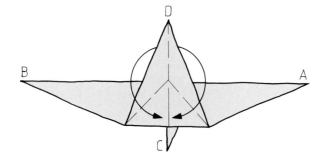

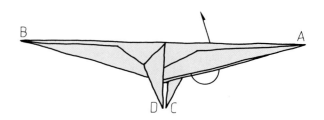

**12** Repeat Steps 6–11 on this side, flattening D to the left.

**13** Swing C upwards, unfolding crease BA.

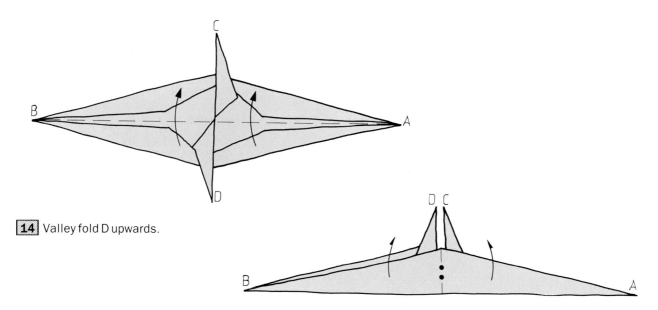

**14** Valley fold D upwards.

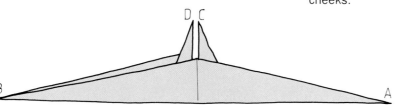

**15** Note that this shape is Step 13 turned inside out. Make a gentle mountain fold down the middle. This will help lock the prongs together and will also bend the Moustache backwards to follow the backward slope of the cheeks.

**16** The Moustache complete.

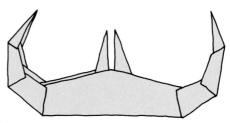

**17** One possible variation is this. A & B are folded inside to blunt the tips. Or . . .

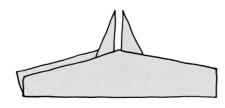

**18** . . . with a series of reverse folds, curl the ends!

---

**CREATIVE SUGGESTION**

*Steps 17 & 18 show two ideas for the shape of the Moustache. Starting from Step 16, invent your own shapes, perhaps altering the placement of the creases in Steps 8–9.*

*ORIGAMI*

# PENTAGONAL FLOWER

This pentagonal design is the first in the book not to be made from a square or oblong. The first nine steps illustrate an elegant way to construct a pentagon from a square. Perhaps surprisingly, there are many other methods. The designer has specialized in folding creations which emerge from seemingly unpromising patterns of geometric creases – see also his Ten-pointed star on pages 142–4. The Pentagonal flower is one of his finest. Its simple crease pattern reveals a flower shape of great beauty – the hard-edged central pentagon contrasting with the softness of the curved petals. Note too how it ingeniously locks itself into shape under tension. Dr Shen folds this design from stiff parchment which begins as a 15 cm (6 in) square then cut down to become a pentagon, but it is easier for beginners to fold thinner paper.

DESIGN BY DR PHILIP SHEN (HONG KONG)

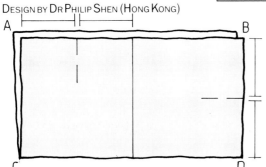

**1** Book fold a square in half, so that the crease runs along edge CD. Locate the mid-point of open edge AB, then pinch the edge at the quarter-point near A. Pinch the mid-point of edge BD.

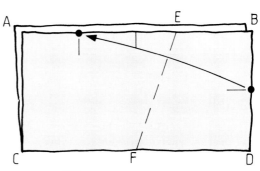

**2** Fold dot to dot, placing the mid-point of edge BD exactly on the quarter-point near A.

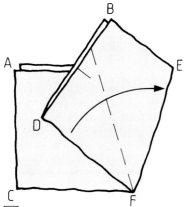

**3** Fold edge DF to lie along edge EF.

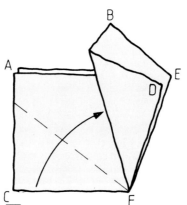

**4** Fold edge CF to butt exactly up against the folded edge.

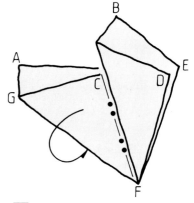

**5** Mountain fold edge GF behind to lie behind edge EF.

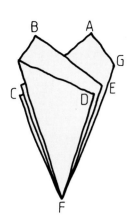

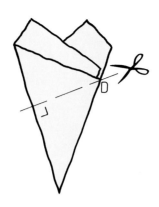

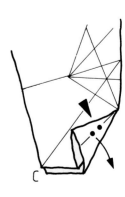

**6** Three edges should line up one behind the other on the left, and three on the right.

**7** Cut in from corner D, making the cut reach the opposite edge at an exact right-angle . . .

**8** . . . like this. Discard the upper portion and unfold the lower . . .

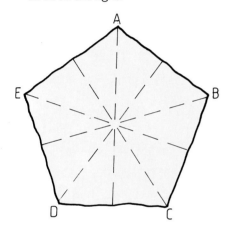

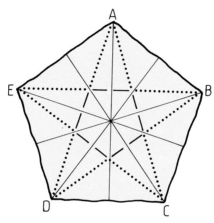

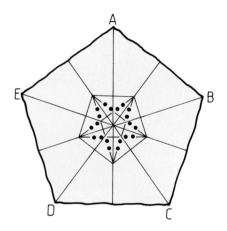

**9** . . . to reveal a pentagon! Crease as shown.

**10** Carefully crease an inner pentagon with five short creases, as shown. *Do not* crease beyond the pentagon, as this will scar the completed design. Take your time! Note where the creases would terminate if they went right across the sheet.

**11** Carefully crease a five-pointed star within the inner pentagon. Once again, take your time and locate the creases meticulously. Note that they are mountains (the pentagon creases are valleys).

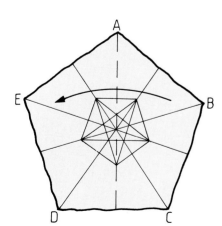

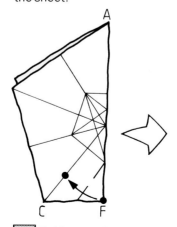

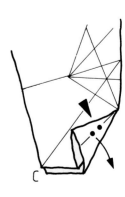

**12** Fold the paper in half.

**13** Fold corner F to the crease running to corner C, so that this new crease touches the bottom corner of the inner pentagon.

**14** Squash F . . .

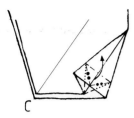

**15** . . . like this. Petal fold, similar to Exercise Four on page 112 . . .

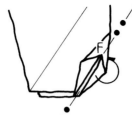

**16** . . . like this. Mountain fold the right-hand portion of the petal behind.

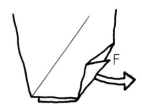

**17** Unfold all the creases to return to the flat pentagon of paper. Repeat Steps 13–17 at G, H, I & J, making and unfolding four more petals.

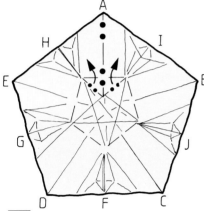

**18** This is the complete crease pattern. Form the inner pentagon with valleys and press in a V-shaped pair of mountain creases from the inner five-pointed star formed in Step 11. The crease to A should be a mountain. This combination of creases will form a wedge-shaped lock . . .

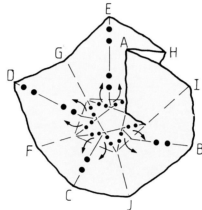

**19** . . . like this. Repeat with B, C, D & E, so that the five locks form simultaneously. It may take a little time to press them all in and then balance them so that they all have equal strength and the paper is a symmetrical shape.

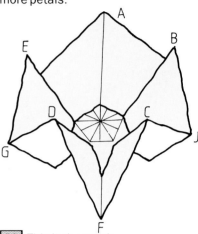

**20** This is the result.

**21** Re-form all the petals . . .

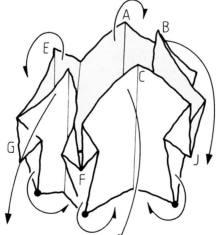

**22** . . . like this, so that each petal looks like Step 17. Simultaneously pull down A, B, C, D & E, allowing the five dotted corners at the bottom to meet underneath. Strengthen the creases in the centre. This will help the paper to hold its shape under the tension now existing.

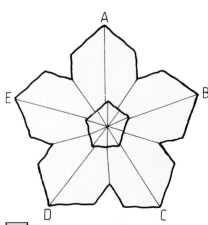

**23** The Pentagonal flower complete.

# PRE-CREASE DESIGNS

This technique is very different to the others so far explained. While squash, reverse and petal folds alter the shape of the paper, pre-creasing merely prepares the open sheet for these — and other — techniques. The distinctions between designs are not always clearcut, however. For example, the Ten-pointed star (see pages 142–4) could be included in this chapter because it is pre-creased.

Pre-creasing is a very common technique, particularly in the USA and in Europe, where the so-called 'engineering' style of folding has its origins. In this style, the sheet is covered with a grid of creases which act as location points for later creases, or which become combined with short diagonal creases to collapse the paper into three-dimensional box-like shapes. The Bugatti on pages 125–30 is a fine example of this technique.

Because of its strict geometry, pre-creasing does not readily lend itself to the creation of animals and other living creatures. It is better suited to geometric shapes and man-made objects or machines. This chapter contains no Basic example or Exercises. Pre-creasing is done on the open sheet, so there can be no preparatory steps or method to learn. Every crease is a basic mountain or valley. It is *essential* that all creases are made with great accuracy.

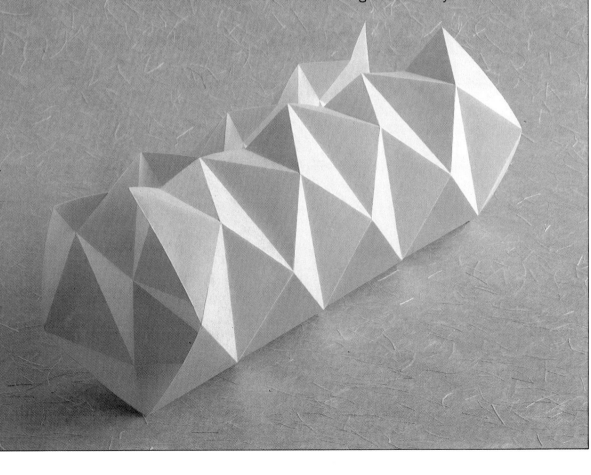

*ORIGAMI*

# BOOKMARK

This is a delightfuly simple design with an unusual pattern of pre-creases. The key stages are at Steps 1 and 5, when the creases have to be formed and collapsed with accuracy. Use a 10-cm (4-in) square of thin duo paper, such as origami paper.

DESIGN BY TED NORMINTON (ENGLAND)

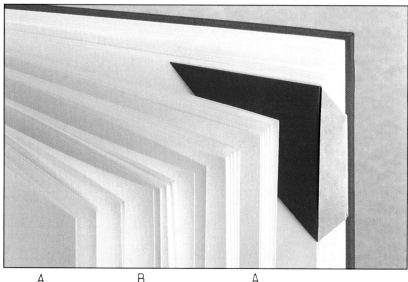

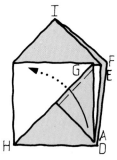

**1** Pre-crease as shown, coloured side up.

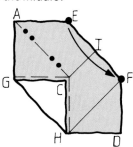

**2** Mountain fold corner B behind into the middle.

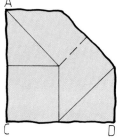

**3** Pre-crease the short diagonal.

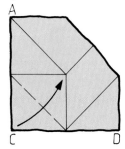

**4** Fold corner C to the centre.

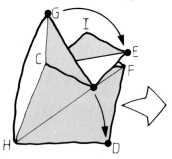

**5** Collapse all the creases exactly as shown, folding E to F . . .

**6** . . . like this. Collapse further, folding A to D and G to E & F.

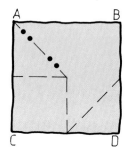

**7** This is the result. Tuck A right up under the white triangle.

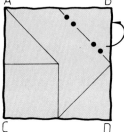

**8** Reverse fold I. Tuck D right up inside the white triangle over the top of A, locking the pocket. Rotate the paper.

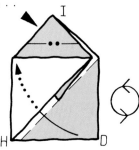

**9** The Bookmark complete. The long diagonal edge below H forms the pocket into which the corner of a page can be tucked. The coloured shape will protrude from the book.

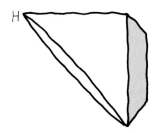

# CUBIC BOX

The conventional pre-creasing pattern of small squares readily lends itself to the formation of box corners, and four box corners can be combined to form a complete box. This design is a variation on a traditional Japanese box. As with most boxes, the choice of paper largely depends on the size of the box and the purpose for which it is being made. The basic rule is that small boxes should be made from thin paper, and larger ones from thick paper, though small boxes can be made from surprisingly thick paper. If no thick paper is to hand, experiment by folding two or three layers of thin paper together.

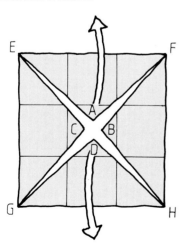

**1** Book fold and unfold two mountain creases.

**2** Valley the corners into the middle.

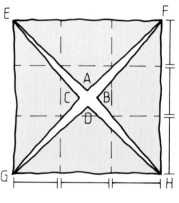

**3** Divide horizontally and vertically into thirds. Unfold.

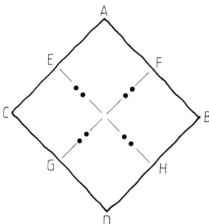

**4** Unfold corners A & B.

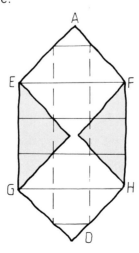

**5** Re-crease as shown. Unfold. This completes the pattern of pre-creases.

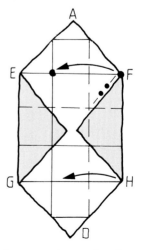

**6** Collapse as shown, forming three separate creases and folding dot to dot. The paper becomes three-dimensional . . .

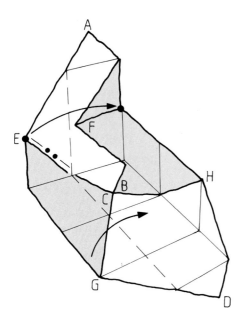

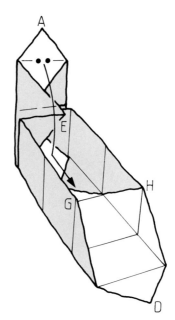

**7** . . . like this. Repeat Step 6, but now collapsing from the left to cover corner F and making another corner.

**8** Lock by wrapping A over the rim of the box, so that it comes to rest on the bottom of the box between corners C & B, as in Step 4.

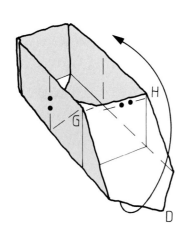

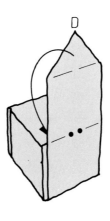

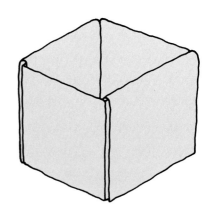

**9** Repeat Steps 6–7 with G & H, then . . .

**10** . . . repeat Step 8 to lock the rim of the box. Corners A, B, C & D lie together at the bottom of the box, as in Step 4.

**11** The Cubic box complete.

### CREATIVE SUGGESTIONS

○ Make a box, then make another but from a slightly larger sheet. This second box will act as a lid for the first. Choose two contrasting colours or textures of paper for the box and its lid. Sturdily made, the box and lid would be an excellent gift box for chocolates, sweets, pot-pourri, handkerchiefs and other small items.

○ The placement of the creases at Step 3 can be altered. By placing them further apart the box will become progressively shallower, though it will still lock in the way described in Steps 6–8.

○ Make two shallow boxes from squares of equal size, but make one slightly shallower than the other (i.e. make the Step 3 creases a little further apart). This will make a shallow box with a slightly larger lid.

# BUGATTI

Even though this is certainly the most complex design so far presented in the book, it is simpler than it looks! The difficult stages are at Steps 1 and 14–16, but they are manageable if you take your time and observe *every* symbol, particularly at Step 14. The other steps should present little difficulty if you have worked through most of the preceding designs. Nevertheless, the Bugatti is a challenge. The pre-creased grid established in Step 1 is used to optimum effect – imagine the problems that would be caused if the Step 14 creases were made without reference to a grid. The design would be impossible! Take each step slowly, remembering to follow the instructions very carefully. Look ahead. Use a 2 × 1 oblong of paper-backed metallic foil, about 20 × 40 cm (8 × 16 in). Foil is recommended because it holds its shape better than paper. The designer has produced a large number of cars, trains and aeroplanes from single pre-creased sheets, some astonishingly complex.

DESIGN BY MAX HULME (ENGLAND)

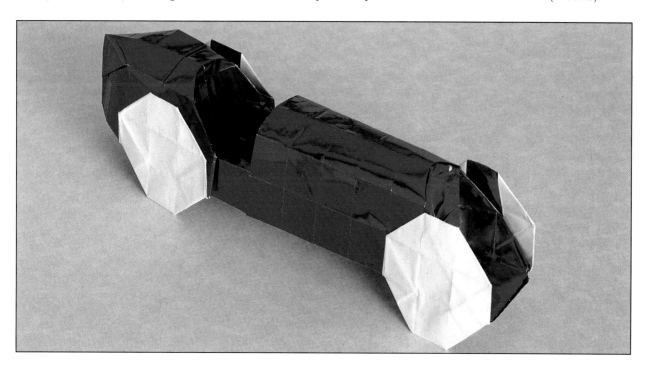

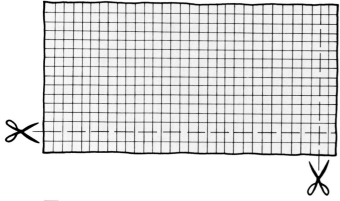

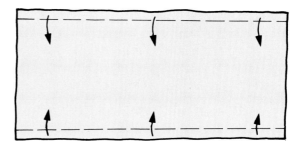

**1** Very carefully crease a 32 × 16 grid of squares, following the system described for the Fan (see pages 38–9) to divide into sixteenths horizontally and vertically, then dividing vertically once more to create thirty-seconds. Cut off two squares horizontally and vertically, to leave a 30 × 14 grid remaining.

**2** Fold in the top and bottom edges along creases nearest to the edges.

ORIGAMI

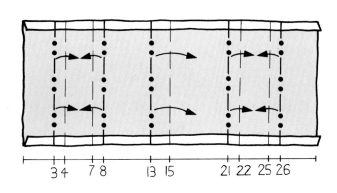

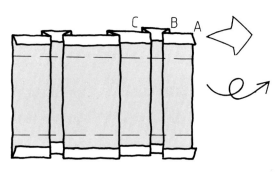

**3** Form five pleats as shown, counting along the pre-creases to locate the creases. Note that the central pleat is larger than the other four.

**4** Turn in the top and bottom edges at 90°, along creases which are two squares away from the edges. Note A, B & C. Turn over.

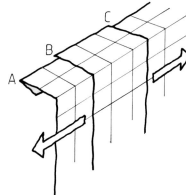

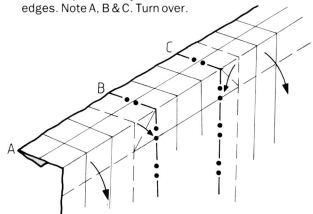

**5** Unfold the two pleats at B & C.

**6** Re-crease as shown, adding a short valley diagonal and a longer horizontal valley at B and again at C as a mirror image of B. This collapses the pleats . . .

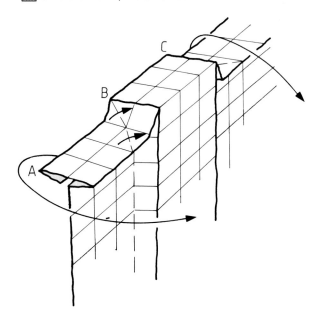

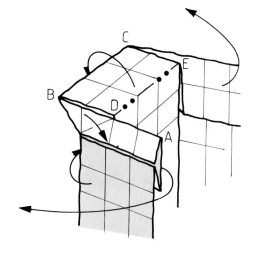

**7** . . . like this. Add a straight diagonal fold across two squares, starting at B, so that A swings across to the right and twists to the vertical. Repeat as a mirror image at C.

**8** Fold BC behind, so that A swings back to its position in Step 4.

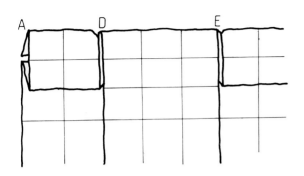

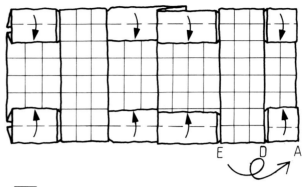

**9** This is the result. The paper is flat once again. Repeat Steps 5–9 on the other three pairs of pleats near the other three corners of the sheet . . .

**10** . . . like this. Fold in the edges between the pleats. Turn over.

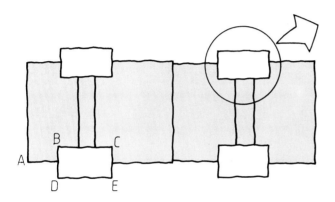

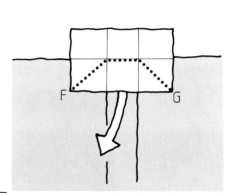

**11** This is the shape so far. The small oblongs become the wheels.

**12** Pull out the hidden layer beneath edge FG . . .

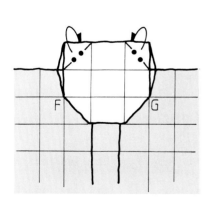

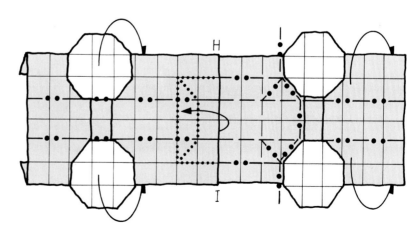

**13** . . . to create an extra portion of wheel, sloping at the sides. Mountain fold the top corners behind to complete the wheel shape. Repeat Steps 12–13 on the other wheels.

**14** This is the complex step! The individual creases are simple to make: the complexity comes from there being so many of them. Re-crease all the horizontal and

vertical creases shown here and add the short diagonals. Note that edge HI *lifts up* to separate the bonnet (hood) from the cockpit. Start to collapse the creases . . .

**15** . . . like this. Fold dot to dot, collapsing the sides of the cockpit so that they are one square high and forming a sloping back at each side of the cockpit, which follows the outline of the rear wheels. At the same time lift edge HI, and *inside* the bonnet (hood) form diagonal creases similar to those at the back of the cockpit. This will form a square box of empty space beneath the bonnet (hood), where the driver's feet would rest. It also helps to square off the overall shape of the body.

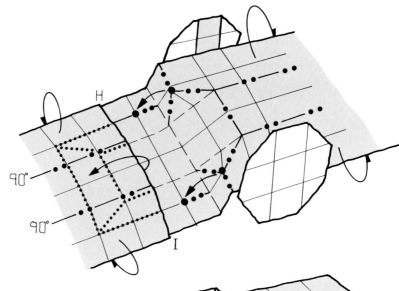

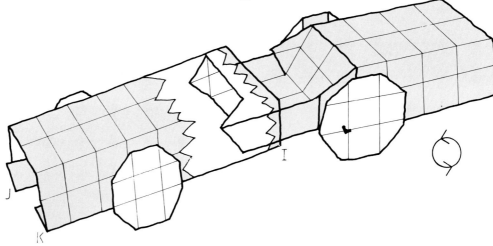

**16** This cut-away step shows the paper inside the bonnet (hood); and the next step . . .

**17** . . . shows the underside of the vehicle. Note the central box shape which is the cockpit. This collapsing sequence is complex but not too difficult if you follow *all* the symbols and arrows. In particular, try to resolve the box shape that needs to be formed under the bonnet (hood) by folding the paper this way and that, and trying to visualize the result. It won't form itself, so try out some ideas if you aren't sure how to do it. Even if they are wrong they will probably suggest other ideas and eventually you will be successful. Remember that short diagonal creases need to be added to the square grid, both at the back of the cockpit *and* under the bonnet (hood) of the car.

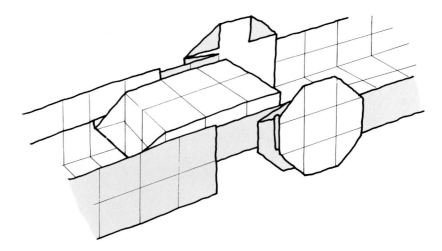

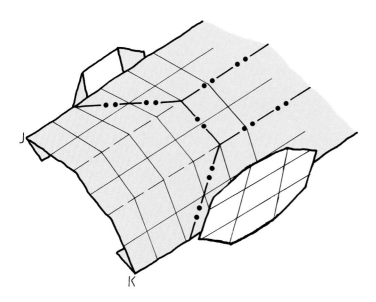

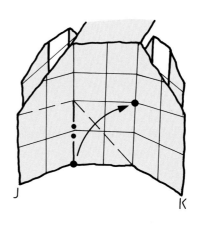

**18** Collapse the front.

**19** Collapse further, folding dot to dot . . .

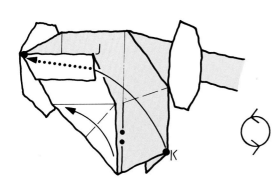

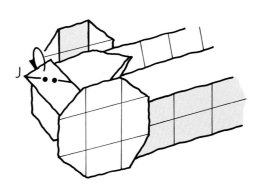

**20** . . . then similarly collapse on the right, tucking K right up inside the pleats at J to lock the front shut.

**21** Mountain fold all the pleats underneath to gather up the layers at the front edge and neaten its appearance.

**22** Collapse at the back along the creases shown, bringing the three dots together.

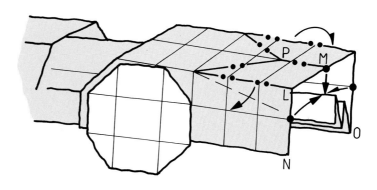

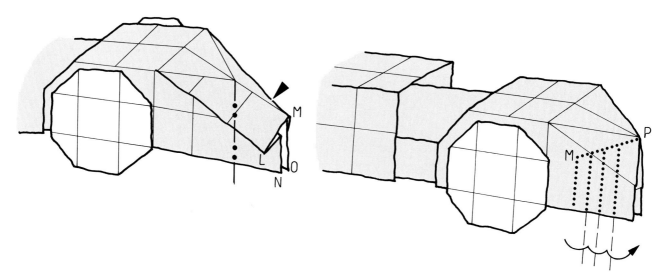

**23** Inside reverse the paper to the right of P.

**24** To lock the back edge, valley fold M over and over back towards P.

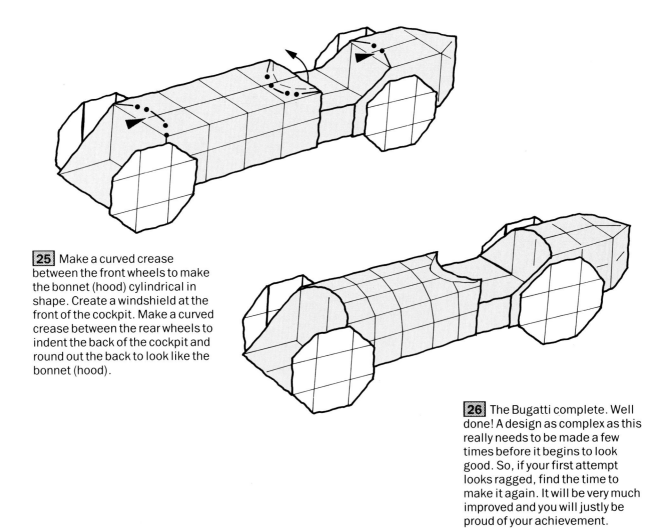

**25** Make a curved crease between the front wheels to make the bonnet (hood) cylindrical in shape. Create a windshield at the front of the cockpit. Make a curved crease between the rear wheels to indent the back of the cockpit and round out the back to look like the bonnet (hood).

**26** The Bugatti complete. Well done! A design as complex as this really needs to be made a few times before it begins to look good. So, if your first attempt looks ragged, find the time to make it again. It will be very much improved and you will justly be proud of your achievement.

# SINK FOLD DESIGNS

The sink fold is perhaps the most advanced of all origami techniques, but with correct preparation and practice it is actually no more difficult than any other technique. It takes many guises, ranging from its classic application sinking the top of a waterbomb base or preliminary fold, to the complex multi-sink of Exercise Four and the eight-sided sink in Steps 2—3 of the Octagonal flower and stem on page 152. This variety is more diverse than, say, how one inside reverse fold might differ from another, and each variation has to be learnt. It is therefore particularly important to fold the Basic example, then work through the Exercises, before folding the designs which follow.

# BASIC EXAMPLE OF THE SINK FOLD

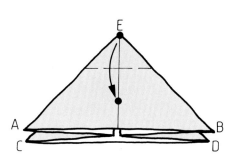 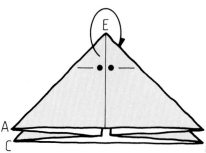 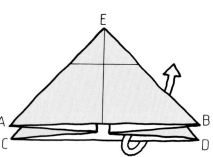

**1** Begin with the waterbomb base (see Step 20 of the Goldfish, page 70). Valley fold dot to dot, creasing firmly. Unfold.

**2** Mountain fold the Step 1 crease, creasing firmly. Unfold.

**3** The horizontal crease should now flex backwards and forwards with equal ease. Unfold the waterbomb base so that point E rises up towards you like a pyramid.

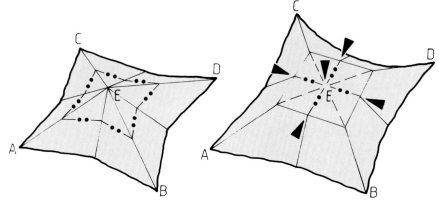 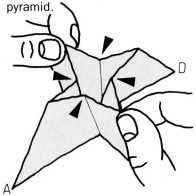

**4** The horizontal crease has formed a square around the centre. Carefully crease each of the four sides of the square to be mountain folds . . .

**5** . . . like this. The centre square will flatten itself to resemble a table top. Change the diagonal folds within the square from mountains to valleys and the book folds from valleys to mountains. Press down on the centre of the square, then push in the sides of the square, so that they start to collapse towards the centre along the changed creases . . .

**6** . . . like this. Keep pushing, observing the crease pattern described in Step 5, so that the square fully collapses. Note how the centre of the square inverts itself inside the lower portion of the waterbomb base.

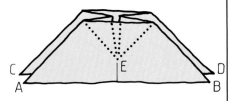

**7** The sink complete. The six steps above can be compressed into 'before' and 'after' diagrams (see the New symbol box). This is how a sink is usually diagrammed.

## NEW SYMBOL

The heavy arrow means: *sink this point.* It is usually linked with a mountain fold symbol, or with mountain and valley fold symbols, if the sink is a multi-sink (see Exercise Four).

When preparing to sink, remember to fold the sink crease backwards and forwards to loosen it, and to change all mountains to valleys and vice versa within the area of the sink.

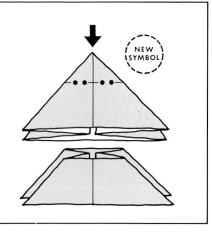

NEW SYMBOL

# EXERCISES

**EXERCISE ONE**

**EXERCISE TWO**

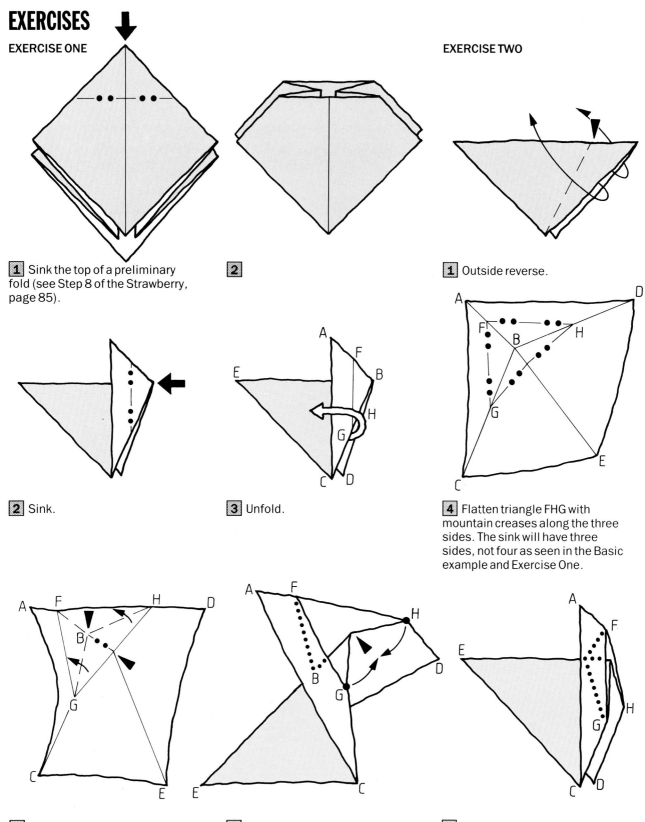

**1** Sink the top of a preliminary fold (see Step 8 of the Strawberry, page 85).

**2**

**1** Outside reverse.

**2** Sink.

**3** Unfold.

**4** Flatten triangle FHG with mountain creases along the three sides. The sink will have three sides, not four as seen in the Basic example and Exercise One.

**5** Form valley creases as shown. Push B downwards into the paper and push the middle of the long edge GH towards F. The triangle will collapse . . .

**6** . . . like this. Continue to push B inside. Flatten the paper so that G & H touch.

**7** The sink complete. In condensed form, the sequence of diagrams would go direct from Step 2 to Step 7.

O
R
I
G
A
M
I

**EXERCISE THREE**

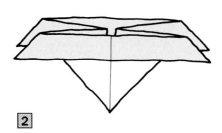

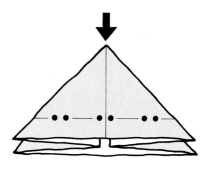

**1** Sink the top of a waterbomb base.

**2**

In this instance, the sink is larger than the remainder of the paper! When this occurs, it is easier not to sink the middle as shown above, but to lift up and outside reverse fold the four edges of the waterbomb base, as below:

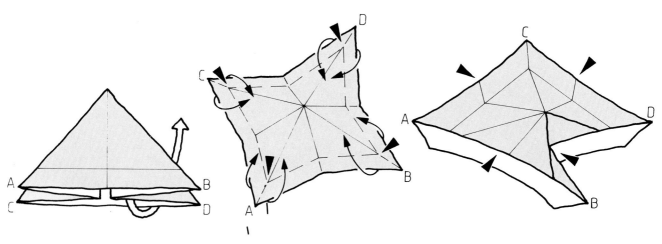

**1** Unfold.

**2** Form a valley crease along the four sides of the creased square and lift up the rim of the paper . . .

**3** . . . like this. Push in on the middle of the four sides to return to a waterbomb base-type shape.

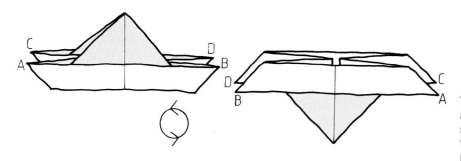

**4** Complete. Turn the paper upside down.

**5** The 'sink' complete, except that a sink has not actually been performed.

This rim inversion technique is also highly useful for complex sinks, such as the one in Step 2 of the Octagonal flower and stem on page 152.

## EXERCISE FOUR

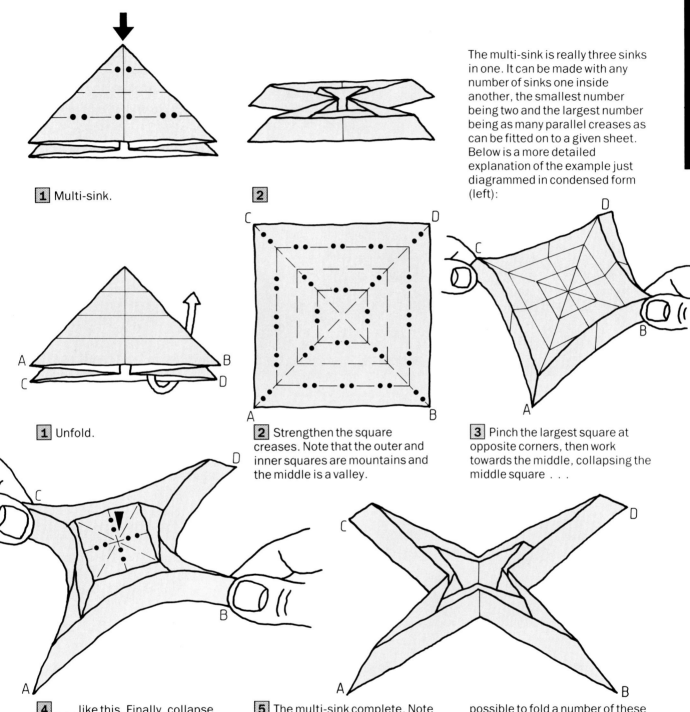

**1** Multi-sink.

**2**

**1** Unfold.

**2** Strengthen the square creases. Note that the outer and inner squares are mountains and the middle is a valley.

**3** Pinch the largest square at opposite corners, then work towards the middle, collapsing the middle square . . .

The multi-sink is really three sinks in one. It can be made with any number of sinks one inside another, the smallest number being two and the largest number being as many parallel creases as can be fitted on to a given sheet. Below is a more detailed explanation of the example just diagrammed in condensed form (left):

**4** . . . like this. Finally, collapse the smallest square by pushing down on the centre.

**5** The multi-sink complete. Note the strong resemblance of each of the four arms to the line of reverse folds made in the Fallen leaves on page 108. A multi-sink is actually four lines of reverse folds, arranged in a square format. The multi-sink technique is an excellent way to achieve long thin arms from waterbomb base configurations of paper. It is possible to fold a number of these configurations from a single square, or 2 x 1, 3 x 1, etc. oblongs, which can then be multi-sunk to create many long thin arms. This technique is particularly useful for creating highly detailed insects, complete with a full set of legs, wings and antennae!

# THREE BOATS

Here are three simple ways to use the triangular sink technique shown above in Exercise Two. The designs look particularly effective in duo paper, but are best made from smallish squares — if the paper is too big the boats become floppy and lose their shape. A good size is 10–15 cm (4–6 in).

THE DESIGNS ARE TRADITIONAL

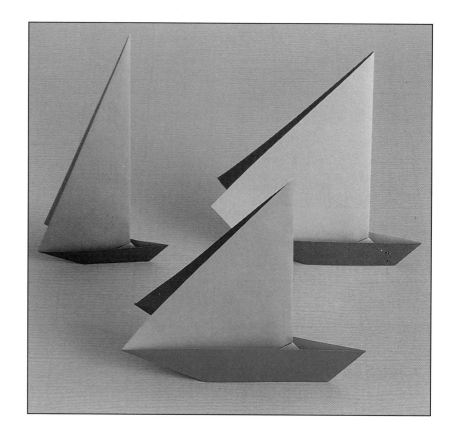

**METHOD ONE**

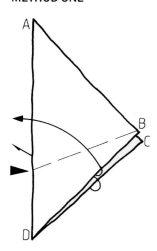

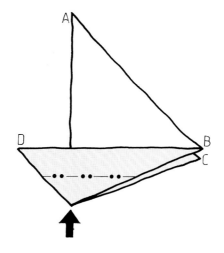

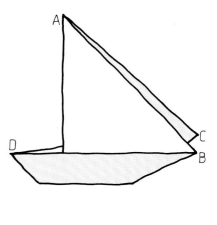

**1** Begin with a square of duo paper folded in half along a diagonal, dark side in. Outside reverse fold corner D.

**2** Sink the bottom corner, as described in Exercise Two.

**3** The Boat complete. Note that it is the same shape as the completed Exercise Two!

## METHOD TWO

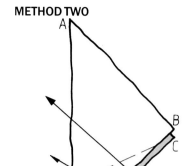

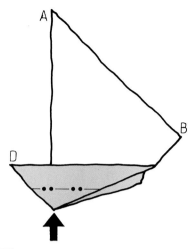

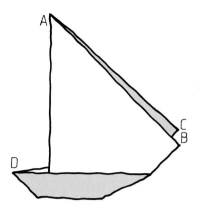

**1** Begin as above, but outside reverse fold corner D so creases do not quite reach corners B & C.

**2** Sink the bottom corner.

**3** The Boat complete.

## METHOD THREE

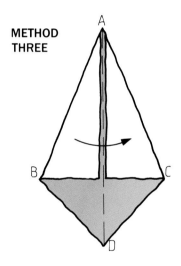

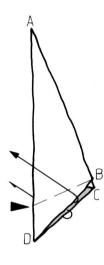

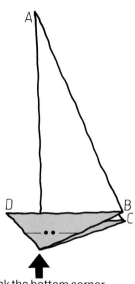

**1** Begin with Step 3 of the Swan (see page 33), dark side in. Fold in half, bringing B across to C.

**2** Outside reverse corner D.

**3** Sink the bottom corner.

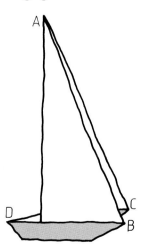

**4** The Boat complete.

### CREATIVE SUGGESTIONS

○ Three sailing boat versions are shown here but many more designs exist. The sinking technique can be applied to many shapes of hull, depending on where the outside reverse fold is placed. Invent your own boats.

○ Create other sorts of boat by pleating and/or reverse folding the sails to make a steamboat complete with protruding funnel, a tug, a liner or a motor cruiser.

# HYPERBOLIC PARABOLA

The basic structure of this remarkable form is 16 concentric sinks, one inside another from the edge of the square to the centre. It is very similar to Exercise Four, but without the book folds which spread the arms into a cross shape. Of all folded designs it is perhaps the most beautiful, combining rigid straight-edged geometry with delicate three-dimensional curves (or rather, the *illusion* of curves), to make a structure which is only ever one layer thick but is immensely rigid. However, its beauty can only be attained with very accurate folding. Steps 1–14 show how to crease 16 concentric squares. Follow this method diligently! It is not difficult, but fold with great care and concentration to ensure that each crease is placed in its correct position and does not stray beyond the diagonals. Use a 20-cm (8-in) square of good quality paper, such as bond paper or any thin paper that can hold a crease well. The design is of uncertain origin, but knowledge of how to distort a plane into a Hyperbolic parabola dates back many centuries. In contemporary origami, the principle was re-discovered by an Englishman.

DESIGN BY JOHN EMMET (ENGLAND)

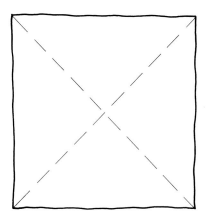

**1** Valley fold both diagonals. Unfold.

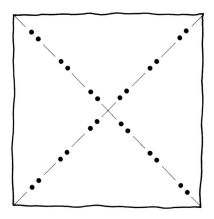

**2** Mountain fold both diagonals. Unfold. The diagonals can now flex backwards and forwards.

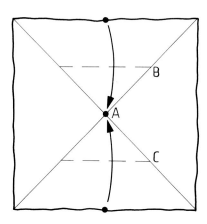

**3** Fold the top and bottom edges to centre point A. Crease *only* between the diagonals, *not* beyond. This is important! Take your time.

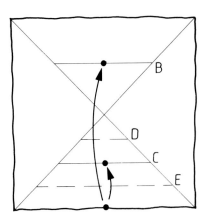

**4** Fold the bottom edge to creases C & B in turn, making creases E & D. Do *not* crease beyond the diagonals.

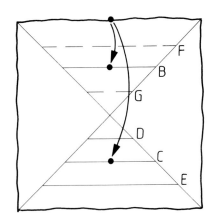

**5** Similarly, fold the top edge to creases B & C in turn, making creases F & G. Do not crease beyond the diagonals. This rule applies to all creases made, so the instruction will not be repeated.

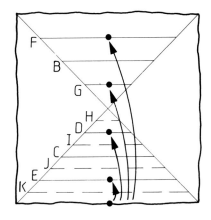

**6** Fold the bottom edge to creases E, D, G & F in turn, making creases K, J, I & H. Keep everything very neat. Crease firmly.

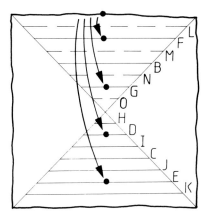

**7** Similarly, fold the top edge to creases, F, D, G & E, making creases L, M, N & O.

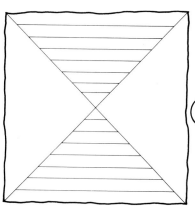

**8** This is how the crease pattern looks at present. All horizontal creases are valleys and are equally spaced. Rotate the paper through 90°.

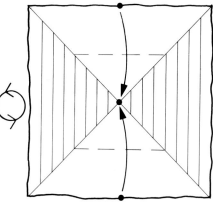

**9** Repeat Steps 3–8 on the uncreased triangular sections, to create . . .

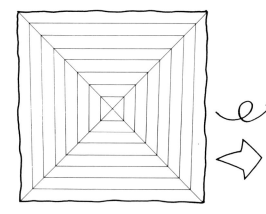

**10** . . . this pattern of creases. Every square crease is a valley and meets another at the intersection with a diagonal. Turn the paper over. (The next drawing is bigger.)

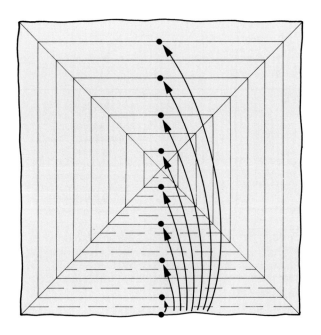

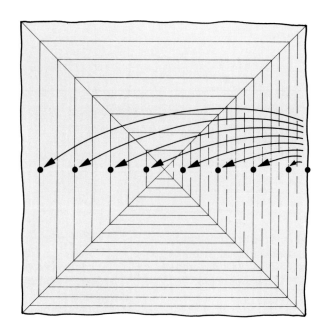

**11** Note that all the existing creases are *mountains* and that all *new* creases will be *valleys*. Fold the bottom edge to the nearest existing crease (a mountain). Crease and unfold, then fold up to the third crease. Crease and unfold, then repeat, folding to the 5th, 7th, 9th, 11th, 13th and 15th creases (the 15th is the crease nearest the top edge). This will fill the lower triangle with a series of creases which alternate mountain/valley/mountain/valley and so on.

**12** Repeat Step 11, but now with the right hand edge, folding it to the 1st, 3rd, 5th, 7th, 9th, 11th, 13th and 15th creases.

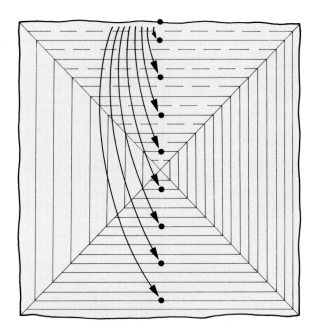

**13** Repeat Step 11 again, but with the top edge. Remember to fold the edge to alternate mountain creases, ignoring the confusing valley creases made in Step 11. Repeat again with the left-hand edge, folding it across to the right, as before.

**14** This, finally, is the complete crease pattern! There are 16 concentric squares which alternate mountain/valley/mountain/valley and so on.

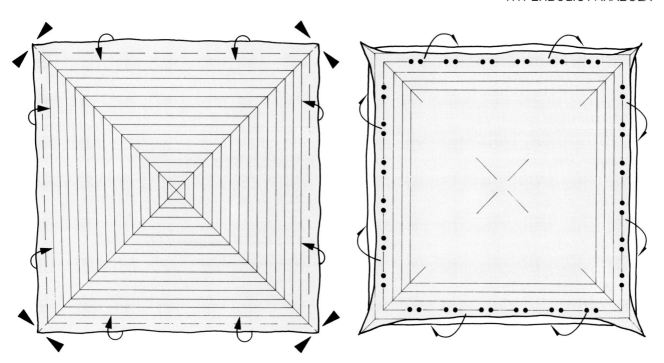

**15** Form the valley creases for the outermost square and crease the four very short diagonals from the corners of the square to the corners of the paper. The paper will pinch at the corners and will not lie flat.

**16** Form the mountain creases for the next square and pinch the diagonal creases as mountains, between the corners of this new square and the corners of the

outer valley square. The effect along each diagonal begins to look like the completed Fallen leaves (see page 108).

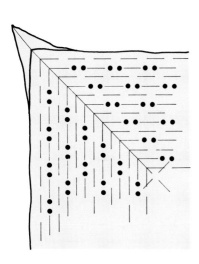

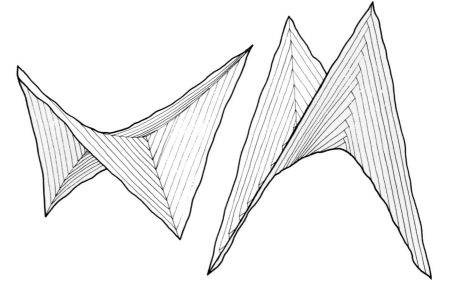

**17** Repeat, forming the next concentric square (a valley) and pinching the corners along the diagonals. Repeat with the next square, then the next and the next, and so on, right to the middle. After the first four or five outermost squares have been collapsed, the paper will start to twist into an awkward three-dimensional shape that will not lie flat . . .

**18** . . . like this! This is a natural contortion: one pair of opposite corners lifts towards you and the other pair bend behind. Don't try to flatten the sheet. The more squares that are formed, the more it will contort, until it becomes possible only to press in the central squares, rather than crease them firmly as was possible with the outer creases. Persevere, pressing the creases into shape with careful finger work.

**19** Eventually, the creases will go in to complete the Hyperbolic parabola. The result will be more beautiful than photographs or drawings can possibly show, such is the elusive three-dimensional structure of its curves.

# TEN-POINTED STAR

The structure of this geometric design is similar to that of the Hyperbolic parabola, in that it contains concentric sinks and has many creases which do not reach the edge of the sheet. As with the Pentagonal flower (designed by the same man) on pages 118–20, the Star is made in three stages: pre-creasing, collapsing and opening out to lock itself into shape under tension. Step 16 is the awkward step, but following the crease pattern carefully should resolve any problems. Use a pentagon made from a 15–20 cm (6–8 in) square of thin or medium-weight paper.

DESIGN BY PHILIP SHEN (HONG KONG)

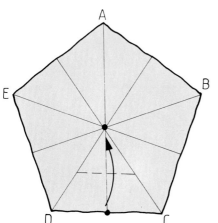

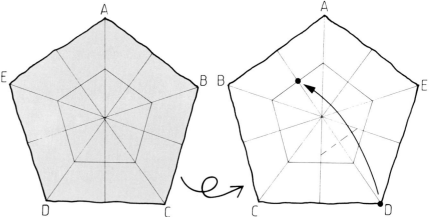

**1** Begin with the method for constructing a pentagon as described in the Pentagonal flower on pages 118–20. Fold the middle of edge DC to the centre point, and crease *only* between the creases running to D & C. Repeat with the mid-points of the other four edges, to form an inner pentagon . . .

**2** . . . like this. Turn the paper over.

**3** Fold D to the mid-point along the furthest edge of the inner pentagon, creasing only where shown. Repeat with the other four corners, to form a smaller pentagon . . .

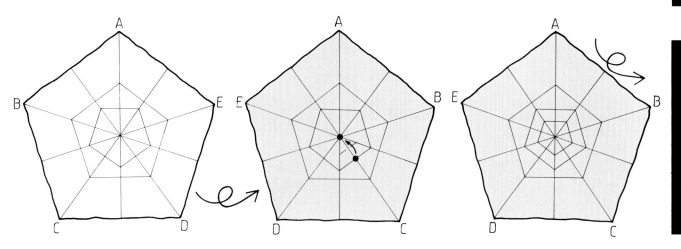

**4** . . . like this. Note that the corners of the innermost pentagon do not quite touch the edges of the larger one. Turn the paper over.

**5** Form a pentagon midway between the pentagon formed in Step 3 and the centre point. It is awkward to make these creases, but be accurate.

**6** The crease pattern so far. Turn the paper over.

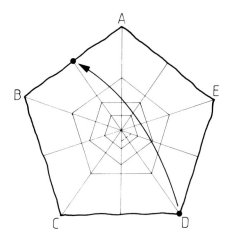

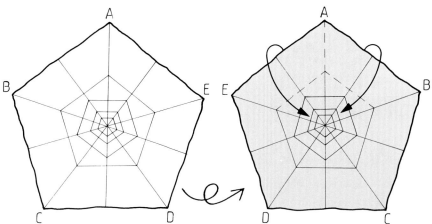

**7** Fold corner D to the mid-point of edge BA. Crease as shown, then repeat with the other four corners to form a very small pentagon.

**8** This is the basic crease pattern which will be multi-sunk. The four creased pentagons should (must!) alternate mountain/valley/mountain/valley from outer to inner. Turn the paper over.

**9** Collapse along creases AF, FH, & FG only, lifting corner A . . .

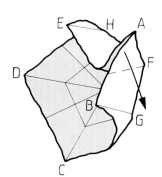

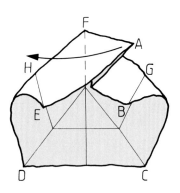

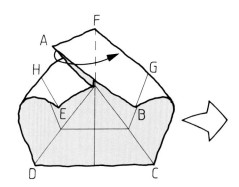

**10** . . . like this. Flatten over towards G, making a new crease. Then . . .

**11** . . . lift up A and flatten it towards H, making another new crease.

**12** It is now possible to lift A upright. (The next drawing is bigger.)

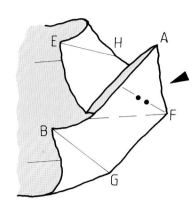

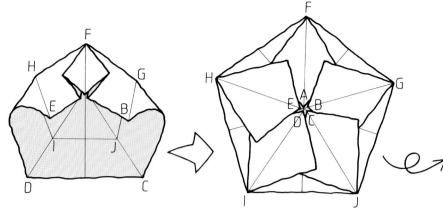

**13** Put pressure on edge AF and squash A flat. Refer back to the squash fold chapter if your technique needs refreshing.

**14** Squash fold complete. Repeat Steps 9–14 on B, C, D & E, squashing each in turn. (The next drawing is bigger.)

**15** A, B, C, D & E are squashed. Turn the paper over.

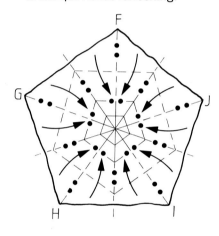

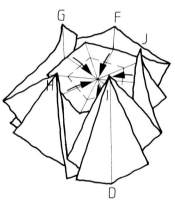

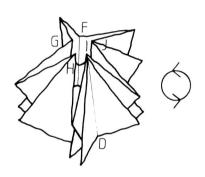

**16** This side is flat, except for the concentric pentagons. Form the valley creases on the largest pentagon, while lifting corners F, J, I, H & G to the vertical. Continue to sink and press the same corners against the middle (mountain) pentagon . . .

**17** . . . like this. Note that A, B, C, D & E which were together in Step 15 will hang vertically below F, G, J, I & H. This Step 17 shape will only form if the mountain/valley pattern of creases in Step 16 is correctly followed. Collapse the final inner pentagon along valley creases, so that the centre point rises up.

**18** This completes the sequence of multi-sinking the pentagons. Strengthen the creases. Rotate the paper upside down.

**19** Note A, B, C, D & E and the other five points between them. Simultaneously flex all ten points downwards and outwards to open the star, while pushing up on F, G, H, I & J to assist the movement. This can be somewhat frustrating, because the Star has a knack of springing shut unless the five mountain ridges that radiate from the centre button are strengthened with considerable force. Nevertheless, when all the creases are strengthened, the Star will hold its shape with ease.

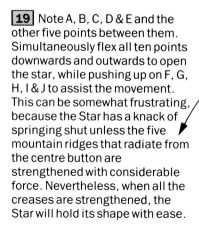

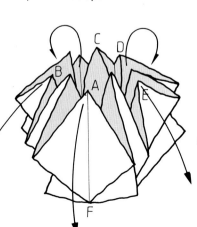

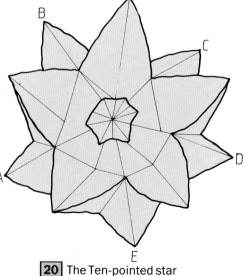

**20** The Ten-pointed star complete.

# PROJECTS

In the previous chapters designs have been explained slowly, so that unfamiliar techniques and the occasional difficult step could be made clear. As a result some of the sequences were rather long. A design that took 20 diagrams to explain could be compressed to 10 or 12, enabling more designs to be presented on the same number of pages. In order to understand these compressed sequences, though, you need to be an experienced paperfolder.

As a rough guide, if you have successfully folded at least half the designs in every chapter, then you are experienced enough to attempt the designs that follow. The compressed sequences mean that some steps include more information than those in earlier chapters. If you have worked through most of the book, you will have enjoyed interpreting the symbols and spending more time on some of the steps should not deter you.

# SPRUNG FRAME

There are many different origami frames designed to hold a photograph, picture or name-card. This particular design has been selected for two reasons. First, because of the ingenious way in which, at Steps 8 and 9, the frame traps the card and the card traps the frame, each holding the other flat, and second because of the way that the crease across the top cannot unfold itself, keeping the frame upright. The proportions of the paper can be altered to suit the shape of the photograph, card or picture that it is to hold. Use thin or medium-weight paper.

DESIGN BY JOHN CUNLIFFE (ENGLAND)

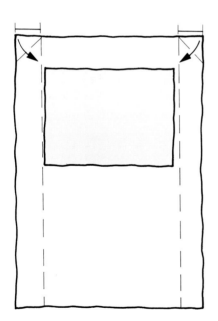

**1** Place the card (or picture or photograph) in the middle of the paper and crease as shown.

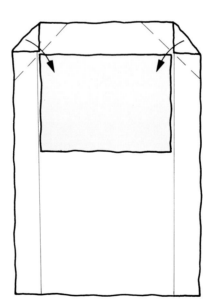

**2** Fold the corners over the card.

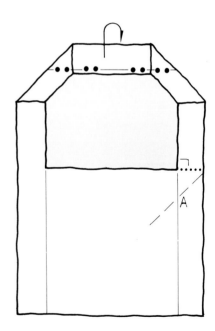

**3** Fold the top edge behind. Locate point A with a diagonal crease.

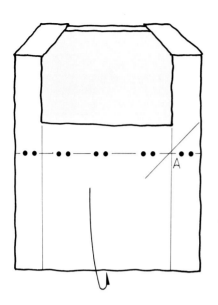

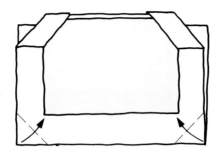

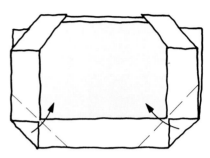

**4** Mountain fold the bottom corner of the paper behind along a crease through point A.

**5** Fold in the bottom corners. They should touch the corners of the card.

**6** Fold over again.

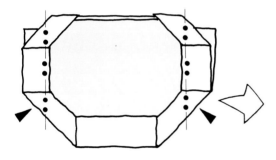

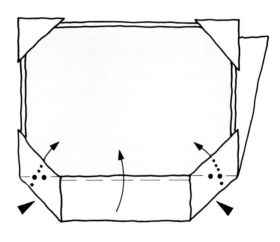

**7** Reverse fold the edges inside, along Step 1 creases.

**8** Reverse fold the bottom edge.

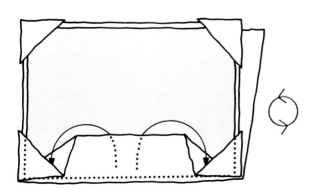

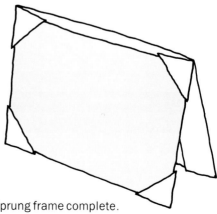

**9** Lift out the bottom edge of the card and tuck it into the triangular pockets at the corners. Turn upside down.

**10** The Sprung frame complete.

# HEADS

It is difficult to capture the likeness of a particular person by folding paper, perhaps because the nature of origami is to generalize. Nevertheless, many origami creators have attempted to fold portraits, often successfully. Here is a system which can create many different heads in a theme-and-variation manner. It may not help you to produce portraits of friends, but it will provide you with a lot of fun trying to invent heads of your own. Use duo paper.

DESIGN BY THEA ANNING (ENGLAND)

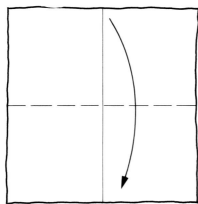

**1** Colour or darker side up, book fold.

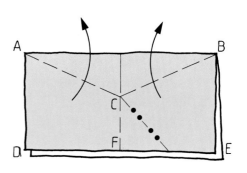

**2** Crease AC & BC separately, then collapse . . .

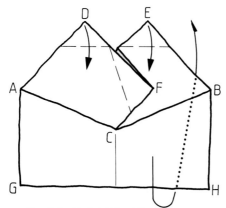

**3** . . . like this. Unfold the AB crease at the back. Fold down D & E. Fold F across.

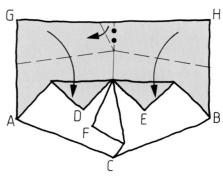

**4** Fold down G & H, helped by a small tuck at the top edge.

ORIGAMI

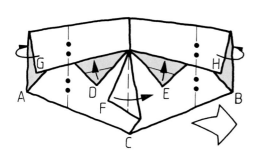

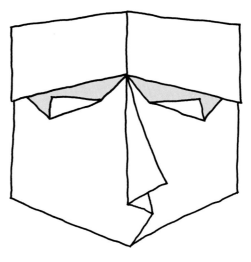

**5** Narrow the sides of the face. Fold up the white corners of the eyes. Fold F back across.

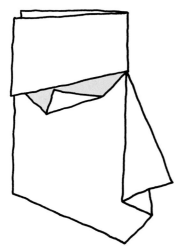

**6** The Head complete. There are many variations. For example, fold in half . . .

**7** . . . to create this profile.

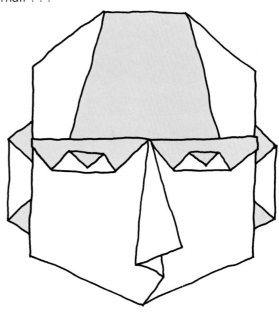

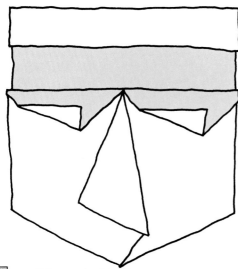

**8** Alter some of the creases to create this balding man with ears, or . . .

**9** . . . this man looking to one side.

### CREATIVE SUGGESTION

There are very many different heads that can be invented using the basic folds shown here. One way to increase the number of new designs that can be made is to change the placement of the major creases in Steps 1 and 2, rather than to change the minor creases made in the later steps. Try also changing the shape of the paper. The square could become an oblong.

# YACHT

Use a small square of duo paper to fold this elegant design, based on a classic mountain/valley yacht by the Japanese paperfolder Toshie Takahama. Note how the eight or nine steps create a design with just three shapes — one each for the two sails and one for the hull. This simplicity captures perfectly the grace of a yacht in full sail. Compare it with the three boats on pages 136–7.

DESIGN BY DAVE BRILL (ENGLAND)

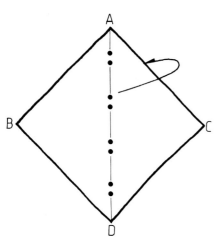

**1** White or lighter side up, mountain fold as shown.

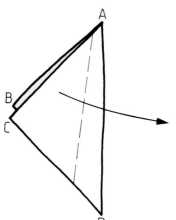

**2** Valley C across. Note that the crease slopes inwards towards the top.

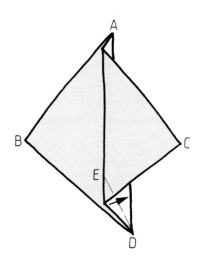

**3** Narrow.

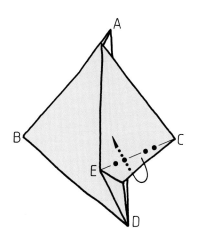

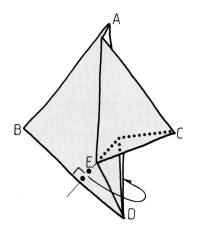

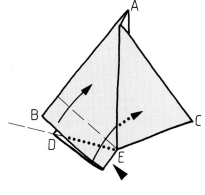

**4** Mountain fold a crease which connects E & C . . .

**5** . . . like this. Fold D behind.

**6** Squash fold a valley crease running away from E to edge BA, narrowing D. Tuck the new corner under the edge above E.

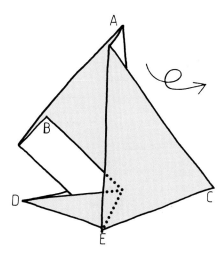

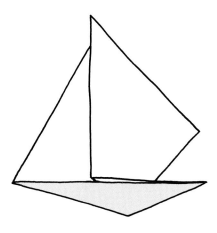

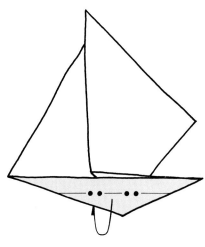

**7** Turn over.

**8** This is the complete Yacht, as designed by its creator.

**9** To make it stand up, fold the bottom corner behind at 90° . . .

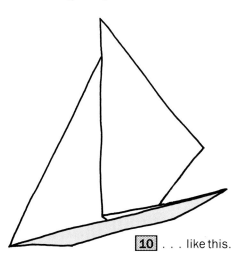

**10** . . . like this.

# OCTAGONAL FLOWER AND STEM

The most difficult part of this design should come at the very beginning! Steps 2–3 produce an eight-sided sink, but made using the inversion technique described in Exercise Three on page 134, where the top is not sunk inside, but the edges lifted up around it. The flower and the stem are folded from squares of identical size. The stem should be green. Use thin to medium-weight sheets of paper 10–15 cm (4–6 in) square.

DESIGN BY THE AUTHOR

**FLOWER**

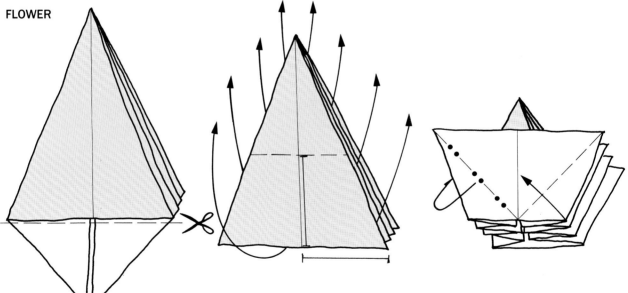

**1** Begin with Step 8 of the Strawberry (see page 85). Cut off the four bottom triangles. This creates an octagon.

**2** Locate the horizontal crease as shown and crease very firmly through all layers. To further strengthen it, fold it backwards, then separate the layers and fold it sideways. Keep separating the layers in different combinations until all eight sides of the crease contain a sharp crease that can become a valley. Unfold the paper to an octagon, then invert the eight edges of the paper along valley creases. Collapse flat . . .

**3** . . . to form this shape. This technique is not easy, but persevere. Valley fold one layer on the right as shown, and mountain fold another layer on the left as shown.

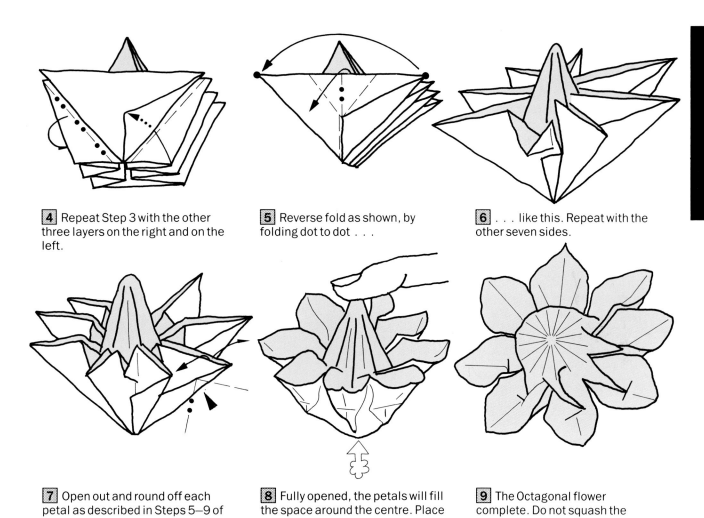

**4** Repeat Step 3 with the other three layers on the right and on the left.

**5** Reverse fold as shown, by folding dot to dot . . .

**6** . . . like this. Repeat with the other seven sides.

**7** Open out and round off each petal as described in Steps 5–9 of the Flower (see page 80–1).

**8** Fully opened, the petals will fill the space around the centre. Place a finger on the apex and inflate!

**9** The Octagonal flower complete. Do not squash the centre flat by blowing too hard.

## STEM

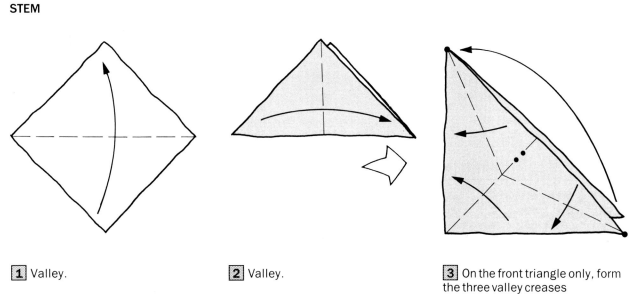

**1** Valley.

**2** Valley.

**3** On the front triangle only, form the three valley creases separately so that they meet at the centre. Collapse along these creases, folding dot to dot . . .

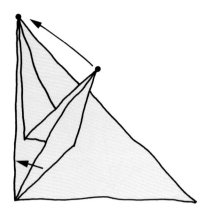

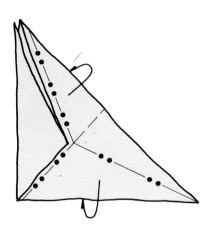

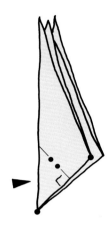

**4** . . . like this. This technique is commonly known as a rabbit ear (three creases are formed within a triangle and collapsed together).

**5** Repeat behind.

**6** Inside reverse.

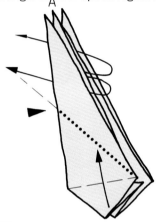

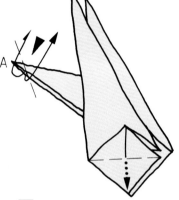

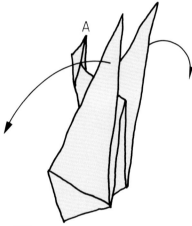

**7** Outside reverse the hidden central spike A. Valley the bottom corner upwards.

**8** Outside reverse fold the tip at a shallow angle. Tuck the corner into the bottom pocket, locking the bottom tight shut.

**9** Curl the leaves.

**10** To assemble, push spike A through the hole at the back of the flower. The Stem with Flower attached will stand in a stable position. If it tips over, alter the angles of the outside reverse folds made in Steps 7–8 of the Stem, so that the Flower is positioned centrally above it. The Flower and stem complete.

**CREATIVE SUGGESTION**
*Make a spectacular display of origami flowers by folding many examples of this flower with the one described on page 80. Wire up the Octagonal flower as described on page 81. Invent a good folded leaf to accompany the blooms.*

# KEYS ON A RING

This is a highly original design and, despite the 32 steps, not very difficult. Follow the steps carefully, giving close attention to proportions, angles and distances, particularly when forming the key heads. Use paper-backed metallic foil – paper is too springy to hold the compressed shapes made in this design. The foil should be a 13 x 1 oblong. A good size is 65 x 5 cm (26 x 2 in), but you may work to a larger scale if preferred.

DESIGN BY TED DARWIN (ENGLAND)

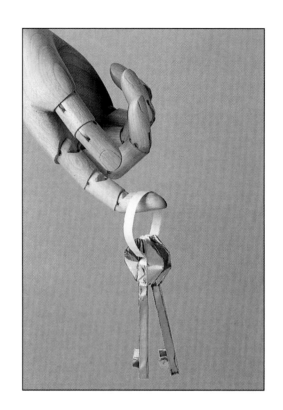

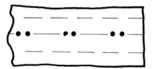 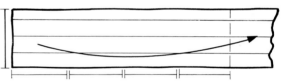

**1** Begin with the strip white side up. Make one mountain and two valley folds as shown.

**2** Fold the left-hand edge across, as shown.

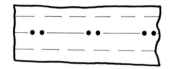 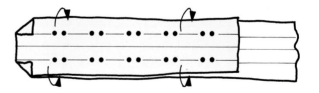

**3** Fold in the corners.

**4** Narrow the strip, taking the rear layer of each triangle behind . . .

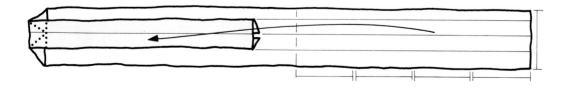

**5** . . . like this. A pretty move! Similarly, fold the right-hand edge across where shown.

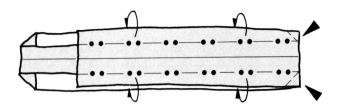

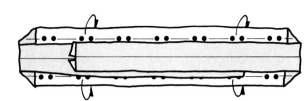

**6** Repeat Steps 3–5.

**7** Mountain fold behind.

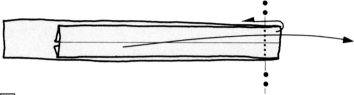

**8** Make a mountain fold on the rear layer so that the top section swivels across to the right.

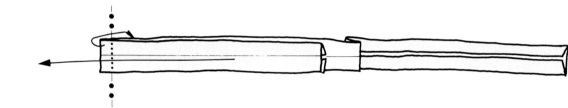

**9** Repeat on the left.

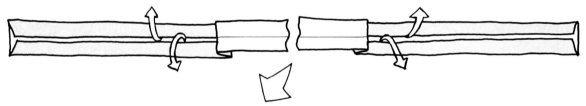

**10** Widen the left and right sections by unfolding the edges. Note: the torn edges down the centre are not instructing you to tear the paper. They are a diagrammatic device to shorten the length of the long white strip

and so condense the drawings to exclude inactive sections of the paper. This device continues up to Step 28.

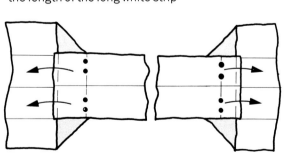

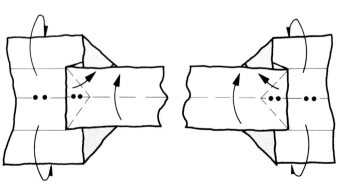

**11** Pleat as shown. Note that the pleat on the left is as wide as a coloured triangle, whereas the one on the right is only half the width. Be accurate.

**12** Valley fold the central section in half, while mountain folding the left and right sections in half and forming V-shaped reverse folds where shown. The result . . .

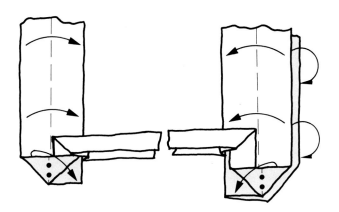

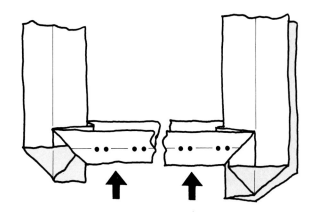

**13** . . . is this. Anticipate this shape when making the creases in Step 12. Sink the central section to half its width. To do this, crease backwards and forwards to loosen the crease, then unfold the central section to push the central crease inside. Refer back to the sink Exercises on pages 133–5.

**14** Narrow the left and right sections, unfolding the triangles.

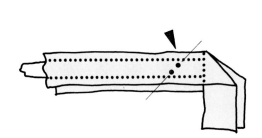

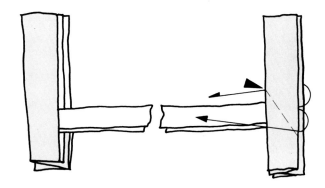

**15** Outside reverse. Note that the white bar is in the *middle* of the crease, not at its top or bottom ends.

**16** Inside reverse, taking the white bar with it . . .

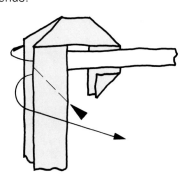

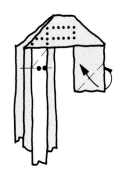

**17** . . . like this. Pleat the white bar. Fold in the ends of the coloured strip.

**18** Tuck the white bar inside the layers of the coloured strip.

**19** Outside reverse immediately below the level of the bar.

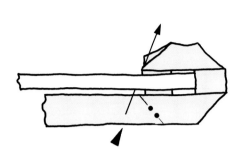

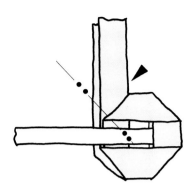

**20** Inside reverse through the middle of the vertical section seen in Step 16.

**21** Inside reverse.

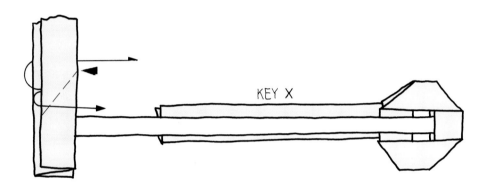

KEY X

**22** Key X is complete. Outside reverse on the left, level with the top of the bar.

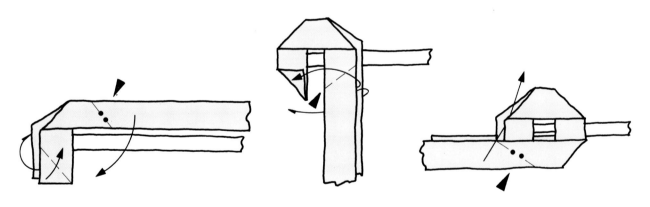

**23** Fold in the ends of the coloured strip. Inside reverse as shown.

**24** Outside reverse.

**25** Inside reverse through the middle of the vertical section seen in Step 23.

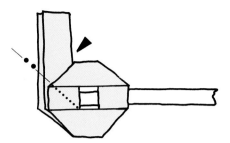

**26** Inside reverse.

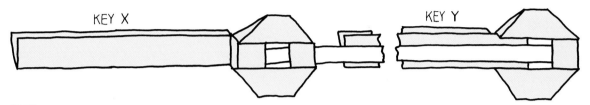

KEY X          KEY Y

**27** Key Y complete. Note Key X to the right.

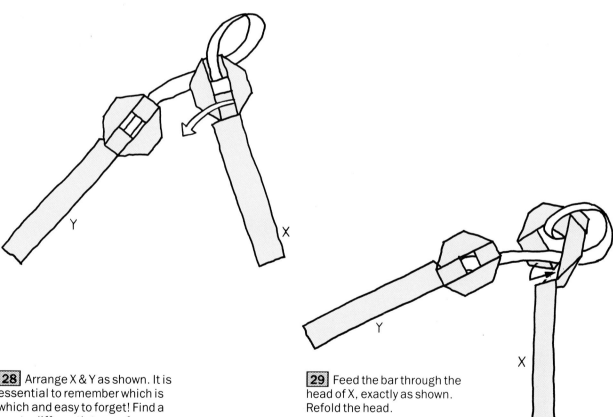

**28** Arrange X & Y as shown. It is essential to remember which is which and easy to forget! Find a way to differentiate one from another. Unfold the head of X (not Y).

**29** Feed the bar through the head of X, exactly as shown. Refold the head.

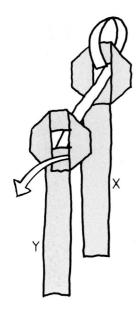

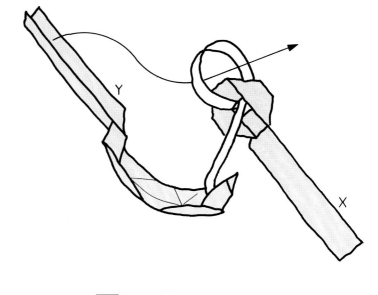

**30** The Keys should look like this. Unfold the head of Y . . .

**31** . . . like this. Push the shank of Y through the white loop behind X, then refold.

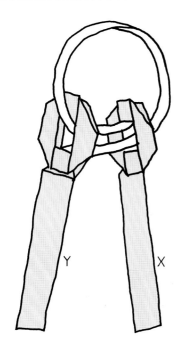

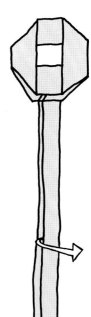

**32** This is the result. If you become a bit lost, start again from Step 27.

**33** Narrow the shank of each Key.

**34** Pull open.

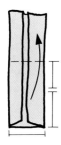

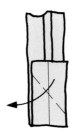

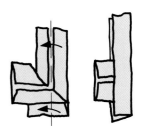

**35** Fold up as shown.

**36** Valley fold across.

**37** Close up the shank . . . like this.

# MOUSE

Compare this design with my own on pages 60–1. They both look like mice, but are very different. Remember, there is no such thing as *the* origami mouse: everyone can invent his or her own. For example, somebody has collected and exhibited over 80 different origami elephants, all made by different creators! Every creator has an individual style and the more styles there are the better. Use a 10–15 cm (4–6 in) square of paper, brown or grey, the same colour on both sides.

DESIGN BY DAVE BRILL (ENGLAND)

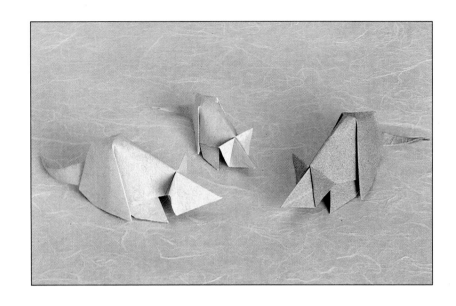

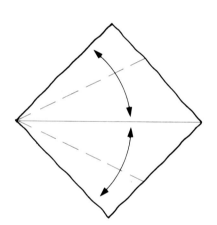

**1** Crease and unfold.

**2** Fold dot to dot.

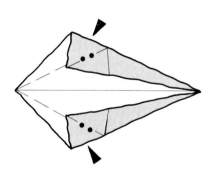

**3** Inside reverse.

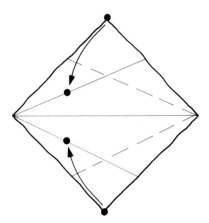

**4** Valley fold across.

**5** Fold dot to dot.

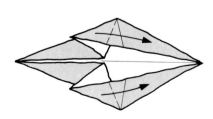

**6** Rabbit ear fold (see Steps 3–5 of the Octagonal flower stem on pages 152–3 for method).

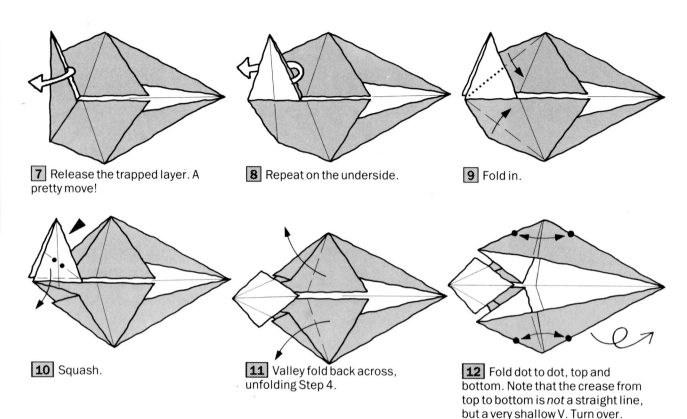

**7** Release the trapped layer. A pretty move!

**8** Repeat on the underside.

**9** Fold in.

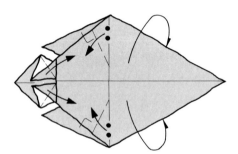

**10** Squash.

**11** Valley fold back across, unfolding Step 4.

**12** Fold dot to dot, top and bottom. Note that the crease from top to bottom is *not* a straight line, but a very shallow V. Turn over.

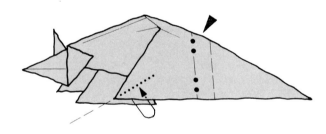

**13** Pleat as shown, top and bottom. Note that the creases do *not* meet at the middle. This gives the Mouse some width across its back. Pull the ears back.

**14** Inside reverse fold twice as shown, rather like making two of the reverse folds in the Fallen leaves (see page 108). Valley fold the hidden layer to lock the rear leg to the body. Repeat behind.

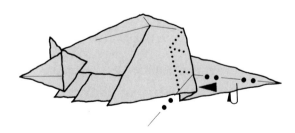

**15** Narrow the tail, squashing the body where shown to allow the tail crease inside the body to collapse flat. Repeat behind.

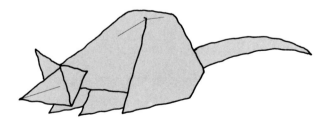

**16** The Mouse complete.

# CASSETTE CASE

Don't be tempted to skip this one just because Step 1 looks complicated. It isn't! It is certainly time-consuming to make, but the results are definitely worth the effort. Fold the crease pattern very carefully and the later creases will fall easily into place. For a full size tray, fold a 4 x 1 oblong of thin paper measuring 88 x 22 cm (35 x 8¾ in).

DESIGN BY TED NORMINTON (ENGLAND)

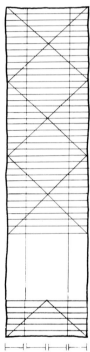

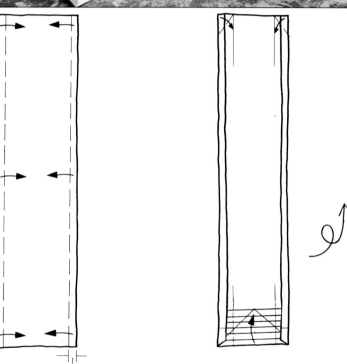

**1** Pre-crease as shown. The strip is divided into 48 equal divisions, including the few missing near the bottom, which are probably best creased. The easiest way to crease 48 equal divisions is to divide into three by measuring, then halve to sixths, halve again to twelfths, again to 24 divisions and again to 48, following the location systems described in the Fan (see pages 38–9). They can all be valleys or a mixture of valleys and mountains, it doesn't yet matter. Crease a series of diagonals down the strip and fold the quarter creases.

**2** Fold in by a twelfth along each long edge.

**3** Turn in the top corners along the quarter creases. Fold up two divisions at the bottom. Turn over.

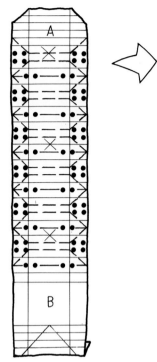

**4** Crease as shown, being careful to keep the pattern regular. Note A & B. The sheet will collapse along the marked creases to form . . .

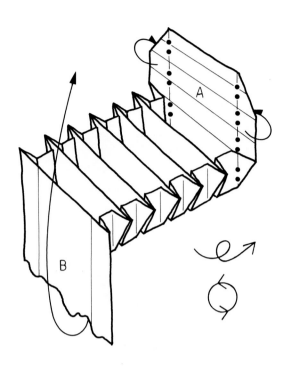

**5** . . . this three-dimensional shape. Note the triangular spikes along the sides of the case. Fold back along the mountain creases at A. Swing B upwards. Turn the paper upside down and move A to the left.

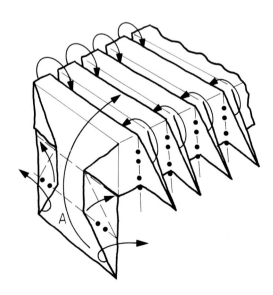

**6** Fold the triangular spikes into the gaps between the compartments. Crease as shown at A, to form . . .

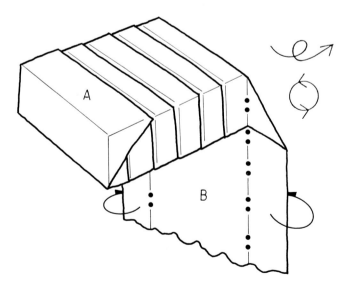

**7** . . . a triangular hood which covers the first two compartments. Collapse along these creases very carefully, following the arrows.

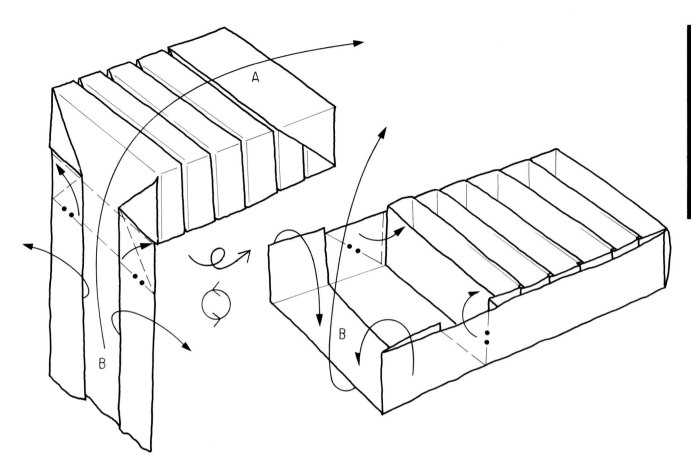

**8** Mountain along the quarter creases at B. Turn the paper upside down and move B to the left.

**9** Collapse as shown, so that B swivels upright.

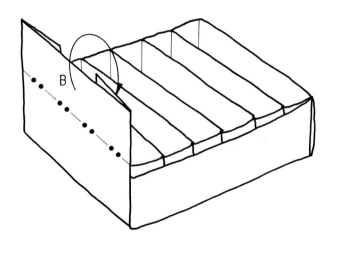

**10** Tuck B inside the nearest compartment.

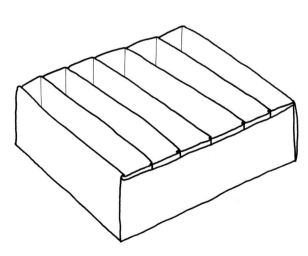

**11** The Cassette case complete.

# SWEET DISH

This is another design made by pre-creasing basic geometric creases and then collapsing them to form the final shape, similar to the Pentagonal flower (see pages 118–20) and the Ten-pointed star (see pages 142–4). The difference is that this design is made from a hexagon, not a pentagon as before. It has an unusual construction for a hexagonal design, because the creases made in Step 10 are at 45° to the edge, not 60° or 30° as might be expected. Use thin or medium-weight paper, beginning with a 10–20 cm (4–8 in) square.

DESIGN BY FRANCIS OW (SINGAPORE)

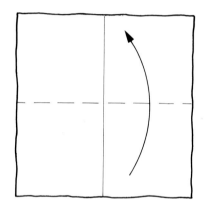

**1** Establish a vertical book fold crease, then fold the bottom edge up to the top.

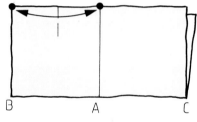

**2** Establish a short quarter crease left of centre.

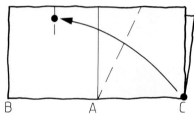

**3** Fold the bottom left-hand corner to the quarter crease, so that the new crease originates exactly at A.

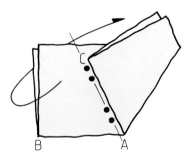

**4** Mountain fold behind.

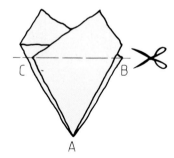

**5** Cut along a line connecting B & C.

**6** Open out . . .

ORIGAMI

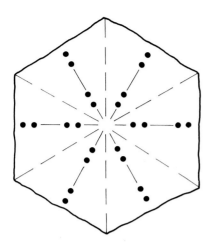

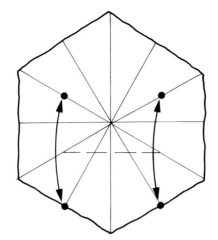

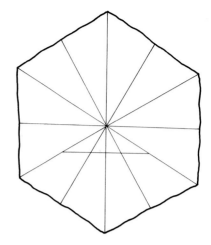

**7** . . . to reveal a hexagon! Pre-crease as shown.

**8** Locate a horizontal crease as shown. Note where each end terminates.

**9** Repeat five more times, to make . . .

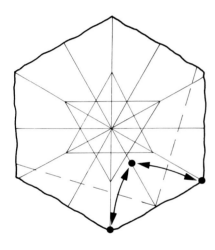

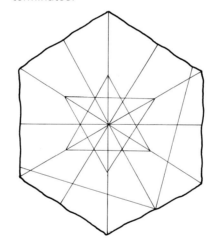

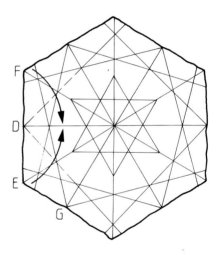

**10** . . . a star pattern. Fold dot to dot twice, as shown.

**11** Repeat five more times, to make . . .

**12** . . . the complete crease pattern. Re-crease at D as shown.

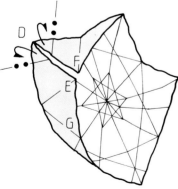

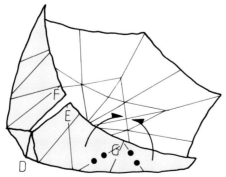

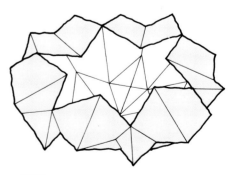

**13** Reverse fold D. The locations for the mountain folds are the valley creases *on the underside* of the paper. Turn it over to see them and strengthen them through both layers to form the reverse fold V creases.

**14** Repeat Steps 12–13 with G, then with the other four corresponding points on the rim of the hexagon.

**15** The Sweet dish complete.

# SPECTACLES

Here is another light-hearted design to add to your fashion collection! For a full-size pair, use a 2 x 1 oblong of paper-backed metallic foil measuring 45 x 22.5 cm (18 x 9 in). Foil is used in preference to paper because the design becomes very thick at Step 11, and paper would unfold itself.

DESIGN BY DAVE BRILL (ENGLAND)

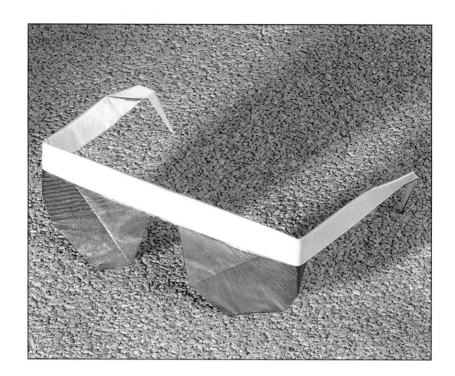

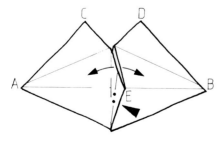

**1** Colour side up, valley as shown.

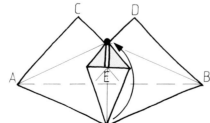

**2** Pre-crease and collapse as shown, so that E stands upright.

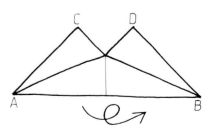

**3** Pull out C & D . . .

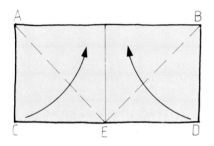

**4** . . . like this. Squash E.

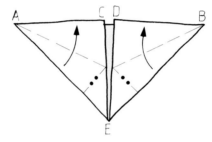

**5** Valley fold dot to dot.

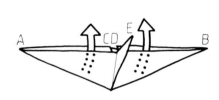

**6** Turn the paper over.

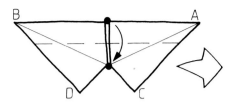

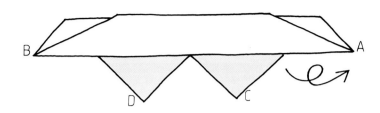

**7** Valley fold dot to dot.

**8** Turn the paper over.

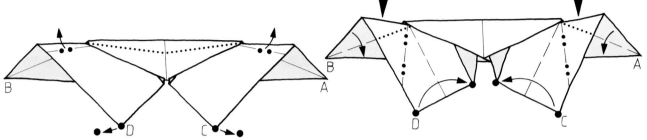

**9** Pull D to the left and C to the right, making new creases at the top.

**10** Collapse the paper as shown, folding dot to dot.

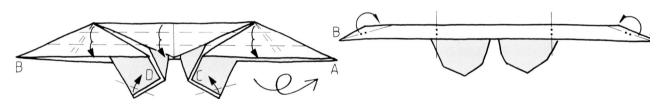

**11** Fold the top edge down twice towards edge BA. Fold in the bottom corners. Turn the paper over.

**12** Narrow B & A. Fold back the arms at 90°.

**13** Reverse fold each arm in the correct place for the ends to fit neatly behind your ears. The position of the reverse may differ from that shown depending on your head shape.

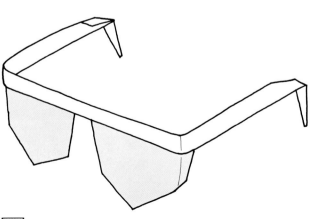

**14** The Spectacles complete.

# SLEIGH

The technique used to make this design is similar to that of the Bugatti (see pages 125–30): the sheet is first covered with a grid of squares to which are added a few diagonal creases that collapse the sheet into box-like shapes. Use a 2 x 1 oblong of red paper-backed metallic foil, measuring perhaps 50 x 25 cm (20 x 10 in).

DESIGN BY MARCUS COOMAN (BELGIUM)

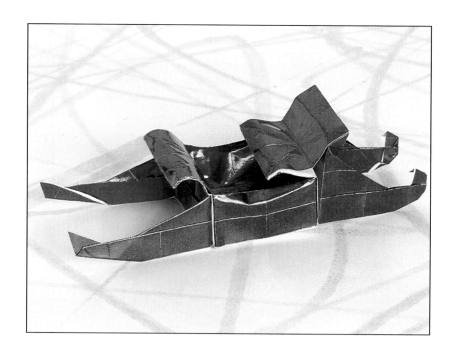

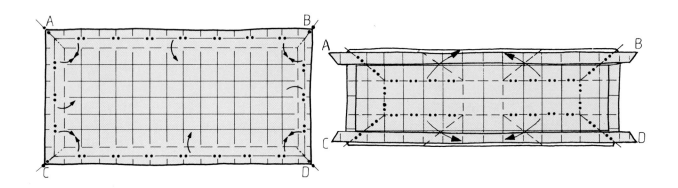

**1** Fold a 2 x 1 oblong into a 32 x 16 square grid, following the location system described in the Fan (see pages 38–9). Make a mountain crease mid-way between each edge and the first crease. Strengthen the first crease to become a valley, then collapse along diagonals to the corners as shown . . .

**2** . . . to make this shape. Make the creases shown, so that the paper becomes three-dimensional. Look ahead to Step 3.

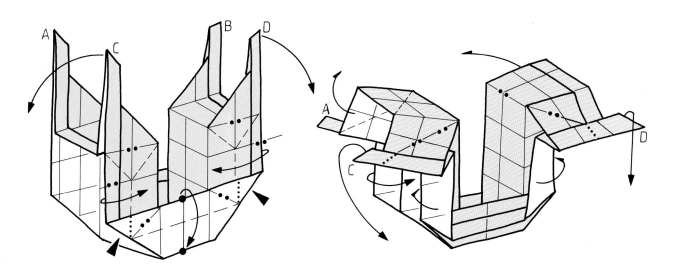

**3** Observe the new creases carefully, collapsing the paper to look like Step 4. Repeat behind.

**4** Separate A from C and B from D, so that AC & BD become straight edges.

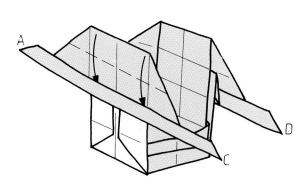

**5** Tuck the top edge under the hem.

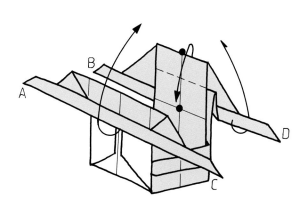

**6** Lift up AC. At the back, fold dot to dot, allowing BD to swivel upwards.

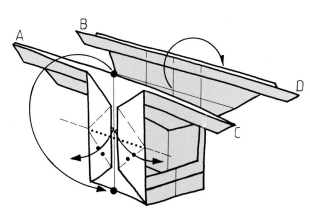

**7** Fold dot to dot, opening the vertical panels with diagonal folds. Repeat behind.

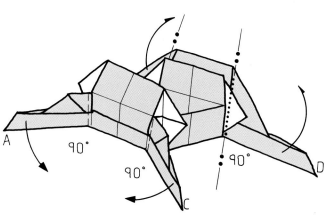

**8** Fold AC & BD through 90°.

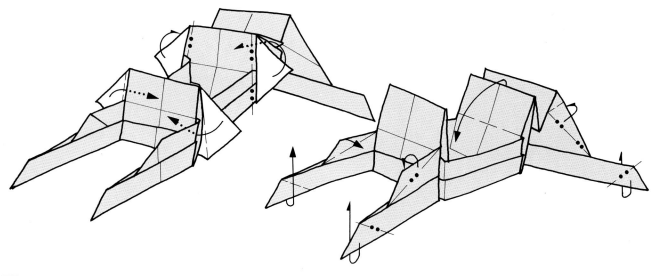

**9** At the front near C & A, tuck the white triangles inside to lock. Repeat near D & B.

**10** Fold up A & C at a shallow angle. Streamline the ledges above A & C. Lower the seat. Narrow the support at the back of the seat and repeat behind. Fold up D at 45° and repeat with B.

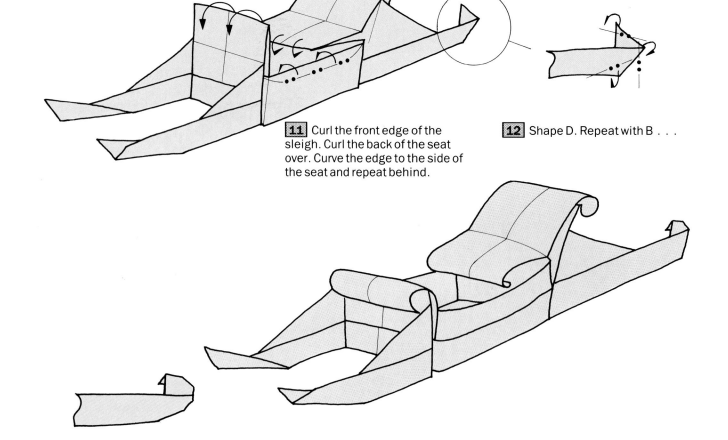

**11** Curl the front edge of the sleigh. Curl the back of the seat over. Curve the edge to the side of the seat and repeat behind.

**12** Shape D. Repeat with B . . .

**13** . . . like this.

**14** The Sleigh complete.

# TABLE OF SYMBOLS

All the symbols used in the book are shown here. Refer to this table when you are folding a design and come across a symbol that you do not recognize. The page number next to a symbol refers you back to the page where that symbol was first used and where it was – in most cases – explained in some detail.

VALLEY FOLD (page 20)                  VALLEY FOLD ARROW (page 20)

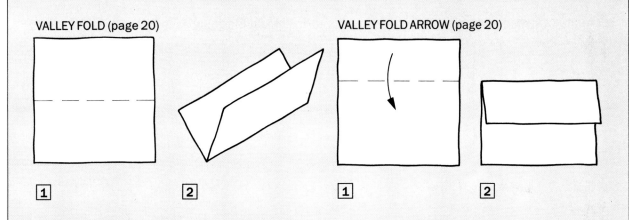

UNFOLD (page 22)                  TURN OVER (page 22)

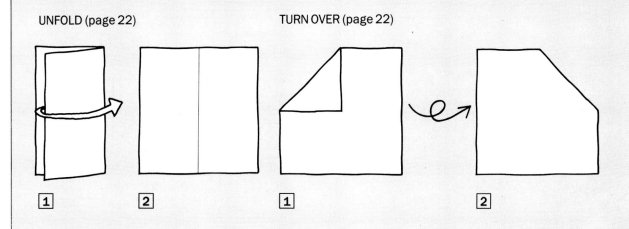

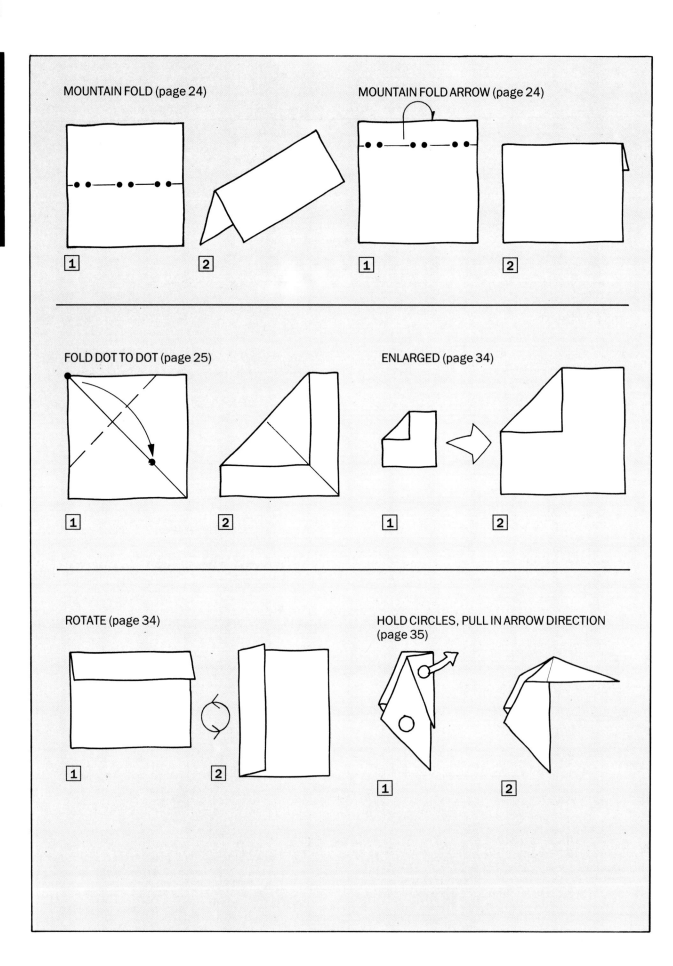

MOUNTAIN FOLD (page 24)

1

2

MOUNTAIN FOLD ARROW (page 24)

1

2

FOLD DOT TO DOT (page 25)

1

2

ENLARGED (page 34)

1

2

ROTATE (page 34)

1

2

HOLD CIRCLES, PULL IN ARROW DIRECTION (page 35)

1

2

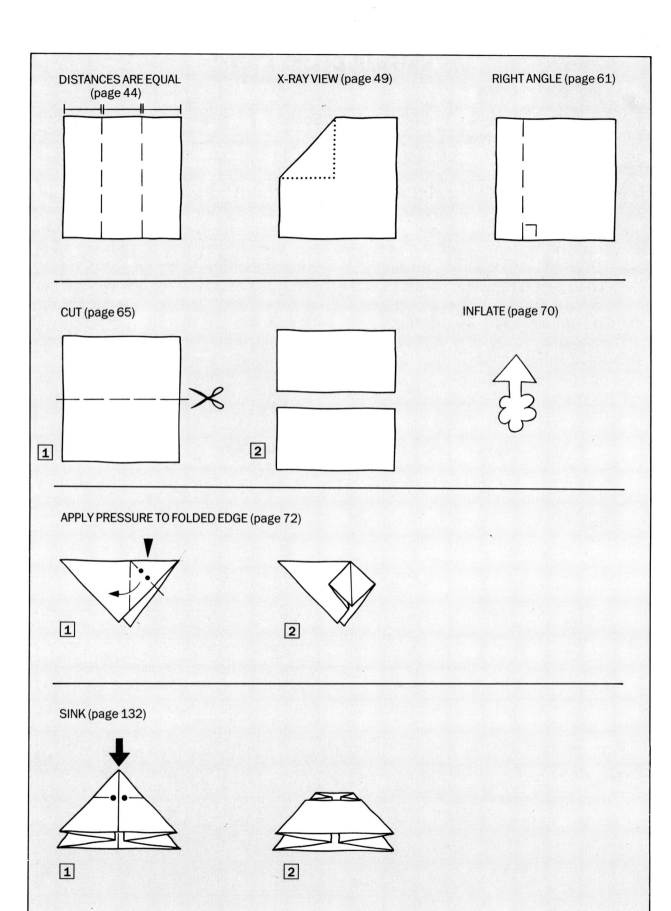

### DISTANCES ARE EQUAL (page 44)

### X-RAY VIEW (page 49)

### RIGHT ANGLE (page 61)

### CUT (page 65)

1

2

### INFLATE (page 70)

### APPLY PRESSURE TO FOLDED EDGE (page 72)

1

2

### SINK (page 132)

1

2

ORIGAMI

# ACKNOWLEDGMENTS

The author wishes to thank those creators whose origami designs are presented in this book, for generously giving permission to use their work. In most cases, the illustrations in the book were developed from a creator's own drawings. The exceptions are: Robot, drawn by the editorial staff of the Nippon Origami Association magazine; Keys on a ring and Cassette case, drawn by Mick Guy; Bugatti, by Dave Venables, and Six Pointed star, by Dave Brill.

Thanks also to Dave Brill, Mick Guy and John Smith of the British Origami Society for their encouragement and support since 1976, and a special thank you to the late Eric Kenneway whose insights into origami so stimulated my interest in the art that it became a way of life and of making a living.

A heartfelt 'thank you' to the many members of the public I have taught, whose reactions to origami and the way that it is presented formed a large part of this book. Their contribution was invaluable.

Finally, thanks to Sue for her patience and support.